Dealing With Curses And Generational Iniquities

Releasing People, Communities & Nations into God's Blessings

Selwyn R. Stevens, Ph.D.

Published by:

**Jubilee Resources International Inc.
PO Box 3, Feilding 4740, New Zealand**

or our secure Internet Webshop at
www.jubileeresources.org

www.Facebook.com/jubileeresources

ISBN 978-1-877463-11-2

All Scripture quotations in this book are from the New King James - New Authorised Version,
unless otherwise noted.
Those marked CEV are from the Contemporary English Version
Those marked GW are from God's Word paraphrase
Those marked GNB are from the Good News Bible

The author uses American English spelling, not the Queen's English.

Contents

Foreword

Based on experience, I have to state that generational sins and iniquities play a much larger place in people's lives and mishaps than most have realized. I discussed this with a friend who supervises over 40 government-employed social workers. He said that this whole concept of how generational issues effect people is now widely recognized in the secular social work and counseling fields he was familiar with.

A huge proportion of the ministry required for hurting people who come to our ministry centre and also to seminars we have run in various countries have included issues relating to curses and generational iniquities.

These issues are not restricted to places like Africa and Asia, but seem common in every culture and country I have ministered. This is also the experience of many I have spoken with who minister widely. I have never heard of a culture that is exempt from these spiritual influences.

I taught the basic material from this book in several places in Africa before I was able to teach it in my home country. The response in both places has been exciting and significant. In New Zealand, we had people attending from almost all Christian denominations, including many from denominational streams not known for their teaching or understanding on these issues. Because of the significant number of scriptures I used, many of these people received a revelation from God, with wonderful responses and freedom for them.

I regard books as paper missionaries that can go to places I may never be able to, so putting this teaching into book form (as well as on DVD) will ensure many others benefit from it too.

Foreword to Second Edition

After teaching about and ministering on personal and family curses and iniquities for well over a decade, I received many requests asking about similar issues for communities, nations and ethnic/racial groups. This second edition has been expanded to cover those issues in some measure. To do these topics full justice would take many books. I'll trust the principles laid out here will lead the serious researcher to a greater understanding in those areas of interest.

Testimonies of lives changed by this material are welcome.

Selwyn Stevens
New Zealand

Introduction - What's it all about?

Before you commence reading this book, I recommend you pray through the following prayer. Please read through it first so you know what you are invited to do, then speak it out loud. Allow the Holy Spirit to add anything else you may require as well.

Spiritual Bolt-cutter Prayer

Dear Heavenly Father, I come to you in the name of the Lord Jesus Christ, and I renounce and turn from all lies, preconceptions, deceptions, self-deceptions and unteachableness that I or my ancestors have believed or entertained. I confess them as my sins and I ask to be cleansed from them by the blood of the Lord Jesus Christ.

I renounce all vows of secrecy and silence about all ungodly activities. I command every lying spirit and every spirit of deception, self-deceptions and unteachableness and any other spirits associated with these sins to leave me now harmlessly on my natural breathing, and not to return to me or anyone whom I love, in the name of the Lord Jesus Christ.

You are the truth, Lord Jesus, and I surrender all these areas to your Holy Spirit who is the spirit of Truth, and whom you promised would lead me into all truth, in the name of Jesus the Christ, Messiah Yeshua Ben Yahweh, AMEN.

Curses Form Part Of Every Culture

A curse is a warning and a wish to inflict adversity upon an enemy, using supernatural powers like a mantra, a prayer or a magic spell as in Harry Potter. (Since J.K. Rawlings' books reveal the genuine curses used in witchcraft, Christians will discourage children from reading her books.) It forms part of many cultures around the world, from Greek and Roman curses to Celtic curses, African American voodoo to the Mediterranean evil eye curse, from German hexing to the Indian shraap.

The Arnstein Bible at the British Library, written in Germany circa 1172, has a particularly vivid torture in mind for the book thief: *"If anyone steals it: may he die, may he be roasted in a frying pan, may the*

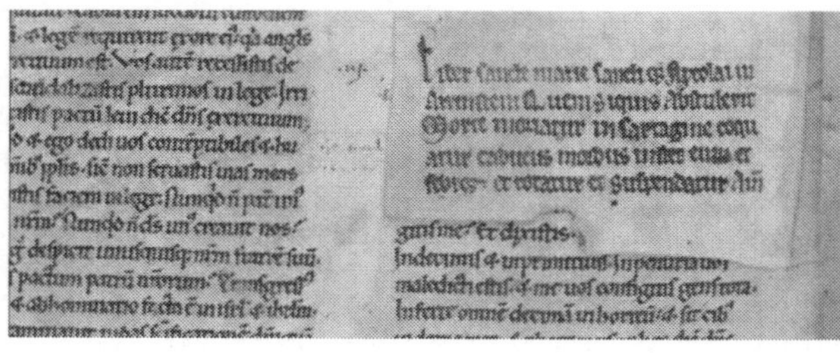

falling sickness [i.e. epilepsy] and fever attack him, and may he be rotated [on the breaking wheel] and hanged. Amen."

Five times daily Moslems globally curse all the infidels - that's every non-Moslem on the planet, Jewish, Christian, Hindu, Sikh, Atheist or Agnostic.

Curses and Iniquities from a Biblical Perspective

We need to reconcile ourselves with the fact that God's blessings are conditional. When we obey, we enjoy. When we disobey, we incur curses. There appears to be no neutral ground. The same God who blesses also allows curses to come into our lives should we refuse to repent of wrongdoing. It is not a coincidence that whenever blessings are pronounced in the Bible, there are curses pronounced nearby.

Curses may come from a variety of sources. Here are the main ones.
1. God – see Genesis 12:3; Deuteronomy 27 - 28.
a. God curses by His Judgments, but in so doing, He never compromises His Integrity, Love, absolute Righteousness, or perfect Justice.

b. Even though God orders the cursing, it can be administered in all the ways available, e.g. by people, nations, angels, and Satan. Satan can't do anything unless God allows him, see Job chapters 1 & 2.

c. God may allow wicked people, Satan, or his demons to curse - 2 Samuel 16:5, 7, 9-13; Acts 23:12; 2 Corinthians 12:7.

d. Examples of God's curses:
* The Four Generation Curse - Exodus 20:5; 34:7; Numbers 14:18; Deuteronomy 5:9;
* Judgment of the Sin Leading to Death - Genesis 8:21; Psalm 37:22;
* Curse on False Prophets - Ezekiel 13:9;
* Anti-Semitism - Genesis 12:3;

* Sin, Rejection of Bible Doctrine - Deuteronomy 27:26,
* Not Loving Messiah Jesus - 1 Corinthians 16:22; Adultery - 2 Peter 2:14.

2. Men representing God – Joshua pronounced a curse on the rebuilding of Jericho in Joshua 6:26, 500 years later it happened exactly as Joshua said - see 1 Kings 16:34.

Another example is the curse spoken by King David on the vegetation on the mountains of Gilboa - 2 Samuel 1:21, and after 3000 years there still isn't any vegetation – a mystery to those ignorant of God's word.

A further example is the fig tree cursed by Jesus in Mark 11 – it was dead the next day.

3. Relational Authority – these can include those in spiritual authority such as fathers, husbands, employers, pastors, etc. There is the matter of Laban's idols, and the curse spoken by Jacob that ultimately cost Rachel her life - Genesis 31:32.

4. Self Imposed Curses – Rebekah took Jacob's curse - Genesis 27:12-17. The Jewish people took upon themselves the curse of Jesus' blood at the trial by Pilate, Matthew 27:24-25.

5. Witchdoctors/Shaman – Including Balaam - Numbers 22. Even an ass was used by God to serve His purpose - Numbers 22:22-35. Balaam was killed for this - Numbers 31:1-8, but his curses were turned into blessings - Deuteronomy. 23:4-5; Joshua 24:10. Even Balaam's name meant ***"Destroyer of the people."*** But God overruled.

A real witch knows better than to attempt to curse a real Christian. Check these out: **"a curse without cause shall not alight"** - Proverbs 26:2; and **"No weapon formed against you** *(the Christian Believer)* **shall prosper"** - Isaiah 54:17; and whoever curses God's chosen people Israel - **"I will curse him who curses you"** - Genesis 12:3. Consequently a curse sent against a Christian who is truly walking with God will act like a boomerang, returning to afflict the originator and leaving the Christian untouched.

Does this mean God prevents all of us being cursed? No I don't think so. God allows us to be buffeted by the enemy for two main purposes. (1) to cause us to repent of and renounce sin and revoke the authority of a curse in our lives, and (2) to train His children in spiritual warfare to defeat the works of evil and to become victorious overcomers.

In Deuteronomy 28 there are 14 verses dealing with blessings and 54 verses that deal with curses. Deuteronomy 27 deals mainly with curses. The emphasis appears to be more on curses than blessings. It needs to be stated that the Old Testament is also part of God's word to us.

Chapter 1 - Curses & Iniquities

The Lord does not want us to be curse hunters - seeing curses under every table or rock. We need to concentrate on the positive aspects of God's Word. But God's promise of blessing, no matter how often it is pronounced on a person, will not be fulfilled fully if there is a curse operating in that person's life. A curse seems to function as a demon directed or permitted to afflict a person. Curses then seem to act as shields or fences around demonic spirits, preventing their eviction until the curse is broken. We may have brought it on ourselves, or inherited it, or through the use of sorcery or other types of witchcraft the curse may have been sent to trouble us.

In Joshua 7, Israel could not take little Ai because the whole nation of Israel came under a curse because of one person named Achan. Many Christians are unable to be victorious in their Christian lives because among other causes, curses may be operating in their lives. It is important first to break the curse so the person can enjoy his or her blessings. The affliction may take several forms.

Jesus read the following Scripture from the Book of Isaiah at the commencement of His ministry. It encapsulates well the primary focus He desires in all His Disciples, from those who heard Him then through the centuries until His return.

> **"The Spirit of the Lord is upon me, because He has anointed me to preach the gospel to the poor; He has sent me to heal the brokenhearted, to preach deliverance to the captives, and recovery of sight to the blind, to set at liberty them that are bruised." Luke 4:18**

We need to begin by looking at the meaning of the terms we will use. According to Strongs Concordance, the term **"curse"** (H2764) means *"a net, a doomed object, a dedicated thing which should be utterly destroyed."* It is mentioned 173 times in the Bible. A curse could also be described as *"words empowered by an evil spirit."*

The term **"iniquities"** (H205) is mentioned some 334 times in the Scriptures, and it means *"to pant or exert oneself in vain. It also means* *trouble, wickedness, vanity, to make crooked."* Iniquity is generational sin being outworked in subsequent generations.

I have heard some Christians say that God is a God of love and mercy, and He wouldn't curse anyone! Such a view conveniently overlooks the holiness, righteousness and justice of God, as well it shows a seriously flawed view of Scripture. The plagues of Egypt were a curse on that nation because of the stubborn rebellion of the Pharaoh.

"You will never succeed in life if you try to hide your sins. Confess them and give them up; then God will show mercy to you." Proverbs 28:13 (GNB)

Dr. Derek Prince likened a curse to a dam that holds back waters of blessing - all you get is just a trickle of blessings plus a lot of problems. The key word: ***Frustration!*** Do you start much, but complete little? Does life feel like you are trying to run through treacle? Do you exert much effort for little reward or progress? If so, these are significant hints you may have a generational curse operating. What do you have to lose by dealing with it?

God expects Christians to live according to Biblical principles. When we do that, no demon or curse may take hold of us. Judas Iscariot was an apostle, but he came under the title of **"Son of Perdition,"** in John 17:12. Because he stole money from the disciples' common purse suggests his life remained unchanged, and sin still ruled him. Ananias and Sapphira were Christians but they allowed Satan to **"fill their hearts,"** see Acts 5:3. (Bible readers will know of these people and the consequences of their compromises.)

Symptoms of a Curse

The following list is compiled by Dr. Derek Prince based on Deuteronomy 28.

1. Mental and emotional disorders.
2. Repeated or chronic sickness (often hereditary).
3. Barrenness, miscarriage and female reproductive problems.
4. Breakdowns of marriage and family alienation.
5. Continuing financial insufficiency (regardless of income level).

6. Being "accident-prone."
7. History of suicides and unnatural or untimely deaths.
(From "Blessings or Curses: You Can Choose" by Dr. Derek Prince)

Any one of these on its own may not involve a curse, although it may. One is unfortunate, two is interesting, three is a pattern. I look for patterns. Several of these symptoms in a family would almost certainly indicate a curse in action.

I was teaching on these issues some years ago in an Australian church. Following the teaching, an offer of ministry was made. Two sisters, in their early twenties, came forward, both crying. They referred to Dr. Prince's list, and through their tears, said they could tick every one of those seven issues in their family. Obviously this would take some time, so I involved the pastor from that church, who together with the girls' pastor, did ministry with them over the following week. Six weeks later, I received a phone call from the host pastor reporting that the ministry had been successful, resulting in no less than 42 members of their family coming to faith in Jesus Christ! I stand amazed at God's grace and mercy.

Christians must be aware that curses are not the only causes of human problems. Problems may arise as a result of our own choice to sin. For example, sexual sins reap a harvest of viral and bacterial diseases, and abortions often result in emotional and spiritual problems. Involvement in the Occult, Masonic and similar lodges frequently has similar effects.

Some people have told me that they don't believe in what I'll call "generational curses." I mean curses in a family that are being passed on from one generation to the next. Yet out of experience I have come to this conclusion: They do exist, not just because I come into regular contact with these type of bondages, but there is enough evidence in the Word of God to support this spiritual phenomena. Generational curses are not 'bad habits' children have picked up from their parents. Generational curses are 'legal contracts' on a person's life reinforced by powerful demonic spirits that don't have any intention to give up their position voluntarily.

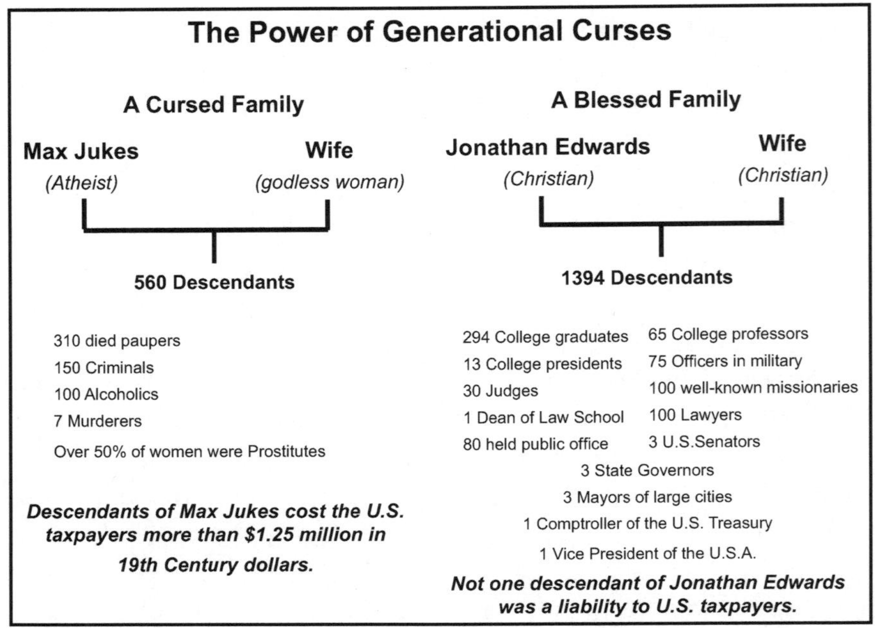

Probably the simplest way to explain these issues is to show you the chart (above) of two families, one godless family headed by atheist Max Jukes and his wife, and the other a Christian family headed by well-known Christian Jonathan Edwards and his wife.

The descendants on both families show the difference between a curse and a blessing.

Generational curses are sometimes the only explanation there is for some individual's problems and for cultural and societal problems in some nations today. Many people in a nation can be held bondage with similar spirits. This can cause a 'national epidemic' that creates bondage as well as the blindness that stops individuals from actually seeing the objectivity of the situation.

The Bible says that these curses will go for at least four generations, and for sexual sins to ten generations. So Satan uses this to not just destroy individuals but to destroy generations of families. It is a brilliant plan – to keep his hold on individuals that have not yet been born! The Lord says that He blesses the generations of the righteous up in a thousand generations. Your children's children will be blessed if YOU serve the Lord.

Whether you're a new Christian, or a person that has walked a long road with the Lord, maybe you're blessed in most areas of your life but there is this one area such as with money, poverty, relationships, the inability to bring conclusion to things, a tendency to fall into homosexuality, or other sexual immorality, maybe you are drawn to occultism so every time you see something on television about 'ghosts, UFO's, spirits etc., you 'have' to look at it.

If you think you have generational curses on you or your family, God has given you everything you need in Jesus Christ to get rid of it. There is a suitable prayer on page 79.

Remember, Satan will test your faith, and try to see if you or your family will still fall for his old tricks. You will need to remain standing in faith!

Like many others, I learned a great deal about this topic of curses from Dr. Prince when he visited New Zealand during the mid-1980's. I recall it was a largely unknown subject prior to then, but both Scripture and life experience connected with the reality of the truth of Dr. Prince's teaching. Dr. Prince mentioned if you wanted to recognize the working of a generational curse, just look at the Kennedy family in America. That comment stayed with me, and I recall mentioning it when I was teaching at a conference in Indianapolis, Indiana, in July 1999. On finishing my teaching, I was approached immediately by several rows of people asking if I had heard the news. They advised that John F. Kennedy Junior's plane had gone missing over night, presumed crashed. The following day's edition of the national newspaper, USA Today, had headlines about the *"Curse of the Kennedy's."*

I always wondered what was the cause of the curses. Then a friend from North Carolina gave me a book with lots of details of the causes of those curses. Entitled *"The Kennedy Curse,"* (authored by New York Times best-selling author Edward Klein) it records that a tragedy for the Kennedy family and their close associates on an average of nearly one every two years.

It began with Patrick Kennedy in Ireland in the 1830's, who was involved in sorcery, divination, drunkenness, bigamy, and who later

died of consumption in the USA in 1858. The author records details of many events by a significant number of Kennedy family members since whose involvement in occultic and immoral (and sometime illegal) activities would, on the basis of Scripture, incur numerous curses into any family.

Other tragedies experienced and recorded in this family include drowning, dying from alcoholism, train, car and numerous plane accidents, death by heat exhaustion, stroke, a failed lobotomy for Rosemary, chronic venereal disease, assassination (J.F.K and Robert), testicular and other cancers, drug overdose, and some were found guilty of rape and murder.

One of the most significant events that would cause a curse is anti-Semitism, a trait most obvious in Joseph Patrick Kennedy. He was the American ambassador to Great Britain prior to and during the early part of World War Two. Let me quote the details: *"...shortly before the outbreak of World War Two, Joseph Kennedy... returned to the United States aboard an ocean liner that was also carrying Israel Jacobson, a poor Lubavitcher rabbi, and six of his yeshiva students, who were fleeing the Nazis. A notorious anti-Semite, Kennedy complained to the captain that the bearded, black-clad Jews were upsetting the first-class passengers by praying on the Jewish high holy day of Rosh Hashanah. Kennedy demanded that the captain stop the Jews from conducting their services in front of the other passengers. In retaliation, or so the story goes, Rabbi Jacobson put a curse on Kennedy, damning him and all his male offspring to tragic fates."* ("The Kennedy Curse," page 15)

Space prevents further details here, but the book does record Jacqueline Kennedy-Onassis pleading with her only son, J.F.K. Junior, not to fly his own plane because *"a Kennedy male dies in a plane crash every seven years."*

A lot of Christians are under God's curse for their Anti-Semitism, mainly because of unbiblical teaching such as "replacement theology." The church never replaced Israel - both are important to God.

Another way to describe iniquity is *"An inherited weakness, bent or leaning towards repeating a certain sin from family activities; or the fruit of inherited sin outworking in your life."*

We all have some attributes we inherit from our parents, including facial features, hair or lack of it, colour of hair or eyes, or mannerisms. Some will also look like an aunt or uncle or some other relative including grandparents. There can also be negative health issues including heart disease, eyesight degeneration and other family illnesses. Medical doctors frequently ask about family illnesses for this reason.

The illustration on the next page shows diagrammatically our DNA - the components we receive from our father and mother at conception. It is the combination of these that brings those familiar eye, hair colour, mannerisms etc. that makes us both unique and also a blend of both our parents and our family blood lines. The way I recall these is the "X" is from your mother because she kissed you, and the "Y" is from your father because he asks why you are home late.

Based on reports from mature Christian intercessors, there would appear to be a third strand of DNA - a spiritual inheritance strand. That isn't going to show up under a high-powered microscope, but can be just as real. This would explain how these work.

An Example of Generational Iniquity

An obvious example from Scripture would include David's immorality with Bathsheeba, with the resulting murder of her first husband, and the birth and death of the baby conceived in iniquity. Then one of David's sons Amnon raped his step-sister Tamar. Amnon was then killed by the step-sister's brother, Absolom - see 2 Samuel 13. It was this same

Absolom who tried to usurp David's throne later on. This is sin repeated by the subsequent generation.

In John 9:1-10 Jesus ministered to a man born blind, and His Disciples assumed that if the man hadn't sinned, then his parents must have caused this condition. That would clearly indicate an understanding of this issue of iniquity in the culture. In that particular case, Jesus stated there was another reason for the man's condition not related to our discussion here, in this instance, God's glory.

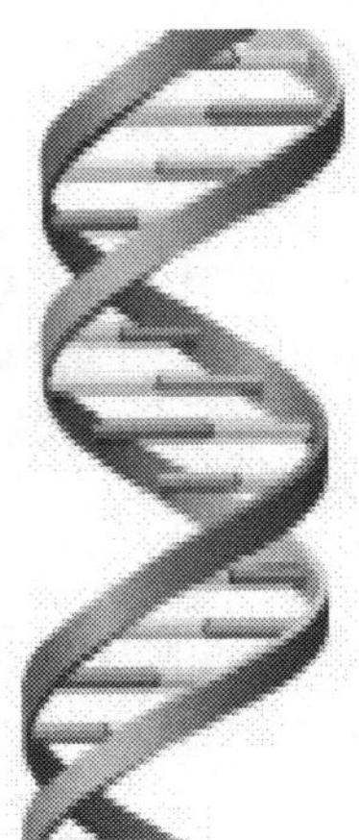

Most people I have met want to be blessed by God. There are conditions for the blessings of God.
1. **Listen to God's voice.**
2. **Do what He says.**

This is covered in the following Scripture:

> **"If you diligently obey the voice of the Lord your God, to observe all His commandments, all these blessings shall come upon you and overtake you, because you obey the voice of the Lord your God," Deuteronomy 28:1-2**

The conditions for enduring curses from God are also clear:
1. **Don't listen to God's voice**
2. **Don't do what He says**

> **"All these curses shall come upon you and pursue you and overtake you, till you are destroyed, because you did not obey the voice of the Lord your God, to keep His commandments and His statues which He commanded you. They shall be upon you as a sign and a wonder, and upon your descendants forever," Deuteronomy 28:45-46**

Some say a Christian cannot have a curse - it was all dealt with at Calvary. That is true: as the following Scriptures indicate:

> **"The wicked one cannot touch us," 1 John 5:18**

"A curse without cause cannot alight," Proverbs 26:2

I would wonder if there is anyone without a just cause for a curse, because none of us are perfect, apart from Jesus Christ.

I believe we need to understand that Jesus died for our sins, so He made provision for our salvation. But yet, not all are saved because they have not appropriated the requirements of salvation. It is widely understood amongst evangelical Christians that to be "saved," a person must repent of their sins, and must put their faith/trust in what Jesus did for us at Calvary. So Jesus made available the provision of salvation, but we must appropriate it in order to receive it. Then we must live out our faith.

Is everyone then "saved?" - **NO!**
God's holiness requires repentance for our sins and the penalty paid. Jesus has paid it for those who accept Him. Those who reject Him are clearly in jeopardy, according to many Scriptures.

In the same way, the breaking of curses was also made available to us by what Jesus did on the cross. The provision is there, but we need to appropriate the provision for ourselves. Jesus dealt with our curses - right? As it states in Galatians 3:13: **"cursed is he who hangs on a tree."**

So, if you are totally perfect, and so your parents, grandparents and great grandparents were too, you shouldn't experience the frustrations the rest of us have.

The breaking of Curses and Iniquities are not salvation issues - they are certainly ***"quality of life"*** issues.

Many Christians have problems and frustrations. Let us check out two versions of a well-known Scripture:

"Behold! I have set before you today life and good, and death and evil." Deuteronomy 30:15

"Today I offer you life and prosperity or death and destruction." Deuteronomy 30:15 (GW)

God is clearly giving us a choice with significant consequences. As many of us have heard from pulpits over the years, we don't break God's word - it breaks us when we disobey Him. Who would want death and destruction? Surely those in their right mind would want God to bless us with life, prosperity and other good things.

While God gives us free will and choices, there are consequences to those choices. If we want God's best and blessing, then we must take some action as the following Scripture shows;

"You will never succeed in life if you try to hide your sins. Confess them and give them up; then God will show mercy to you," Proverbs 28:13. (GNB)

Parents can and do say things to their children, both good and bad, but many don't realize the effects of what they have been saying. I recall in younger days going out with a nice young woman when I was single. On one occasion she took me to meet her parents and siblings for afternoon tea. I noticed all the family members had "coke bottle glasses" with very thick lenses. We had a pleasant visit until one of the younger brothers accidentally knocked over his soft drink on the kitchen table. Without a moment's hesitation, the father stated, *"Oh, curse your eyes."* This family originated from Scotland, and the Scots are well-known for cursing each other, especially those belonging to other clans. Most cultures also have this practice, although some are more practised than others.

Historically there is evidence the Druid priests did this with occultic curse songs against the Roman occupying military in England, causing many unpleasant boils to break out under their leather tunics that must have been most uncomfortable and also caused many deaths.

The Vietnam War Curse

A former Vietnamese Buddhist monk has confessed that an entire sect of Buddhist monks spent much of the Vietnam War cursing all foreign military servicemen in their country. They took shifts at the end of the military airport runway through which all foreign military personnel entered Vietnam during the war. The curses were specific - a very powerful witchcraft curse with three parts:

1. That the foreign soldiers would become wandering men and women for the rest of their lives;

2 That they would never find peace; and

3. That they would be angry men and women for the rest of their lives. (Source:"The Unseen War:Allies Ambushed" p 8, by Pointman International Ministries - available from Jubilee Resources.)

Psychiatrists and doctors gave it a name - *"Post Traumatic Stress Disorder."* They admit they have no solution, apart from heavy drug medications. I mentioned this Buddhist curse during a teaching session with 200 trainee counselors in Melbourne Australia some years ago. Following that session a man came forward, and after introducing himself he said he had been a Christian all his adult life, yet with tears in his eyes, he stated that I had just described the past 25 years of his life, following his military service in Vietnam. Ministry was arranged for him immediately. Several other men who were also in Vietnam have also responded and been set free.

Other Examples

Islamic Mullahs (priests) from Iraq and Saudi Arabia prayed similar curses against American and other coalition military members during the Gulf Wars. Many Islamic Mullahs, during the five times for prayer daily, frequently curse all the "Infidels" - Christians, Jews, Hindus, Sikhs, Atheists, Agnostics and any other non-Moslems.

Former Israeli Prime Minister, Ariel Sharon, was taken to hospital with a severe stroke in 2006. Occultists within Judaism signed a death curse on him only a week prior to the stroke because of his leadership role in pulling the Israeli military out from the Gaza Strip after many years of Israeli military occupation. Gaza originally belonged to the Philistines, and there has always been a very strong occultic and contentious spiritual strongman/principality over that region. When the leaders of nations are ignorant of the spiritual realm, these are the expected results. Sharon was in the coma for about seven years prior to dying in 2014. He never regained consciousness.

Knowledge about the specific nature of such curses is very helpful when breaking them off. Before you do any ministry with someone related to these issues raised above. Chapter 14 and Appendix 1 on pages 78-81 have the ministry suggestions we recommend.

I believe there are twelve primary curses mentioned in Scripture preventing many Christians coming into the fullness of the God's blessings. Let us have a look at these now.

Chapter 2
Power of Spoken Words

There's an old saying that I learned when I was growing up. You may remember it. *"Sticks and stones may break my bones, but names will never hurt me."* The problem is it's not true - names can hurt. I remember a situation many years ago, where the mother of a 12-year-old girl told her that since she would never amount to anything, and in order to prevent her coming home pregnant, had her daughter injected with a chemical to prevent pregnancy. The daughter was a particularly attractive young woman, but because her mother's expectations were so low, she was every teenage boy's plaything in that town. She had a rather crude nickname as a result. But a Christian couple who owned a business in that town saw something special in that young woman and gave her a job when she was old enough to work. They began to teach her by word and example that she was much more precious than her mother had told her. It didn't take very long to break the pattern of promiscuity. She blossomed as a human being, and her life was totally changed. Her mother's words and actions put an expectation that was too low and are effectively a curse; but the Christian couple saw her value as a human being, made in the image of God, and broke the curse through love, witness and ministry.

> **"But I say to you that every idle word, whatever men may speak, they shall give account of it in the Day of Judgment. For by your words you shall be justified, and by your words you shall be condemned." Matthew 12:36-37**

The most powerful curses are spoken words. On some occasions we say these things against ourselves. Sometimes we call these "Rash Vows." I always caution people to never say "never" - *"I'll **never** shop there again because of the rudeness of the staff,"* or *"I'll **never** be like my mother..."* The issue is that if you do shop there when you have forgotten about your words, or mimic your mother in some action or mannerism, those words now empowered by the spiritual realm, will now begin to work against you, and cause frustration - they can indeed become a curse.

Another Scripture, that is probably the key verse for us to remember from this section is found in:

"Death and life are in the power of the tongue, and those who love it shall eat the fruit of it." Proverbs 18:21

A woman I know decided to test this out. She cooked a pot of rice, and when it cooled put half the rice in each jar, and then placed them in different cupboards. She then spoke daily to the contents of each jar for two months. You can see the difference. The blessed rice stayed creamy colored, the cursed one turned an unhealthy brown. She's convinced now, and is teaching her family about the power in words.

Let's have some examples from Scripture, that will help illustrate the power of curses in the lives of real people.

* David cursed the mountains of Gilboa because of the treachery of those people, and to this day, about 3000 years later, there is still no vegetation growing on these mountains.

"Mountains of Gilboa, may you neither have dew nor rain, nor fields that yield of offerings of grain. For there the shield of the mighty was defiled, the shield of Saul - no longer rubbed (anointed) with oil." 2 Samuel 1:21 (NIV)

* Following the destruction of Jericho, Joshua cursed the family who ever rebuilt that city. So here are his words, followed by the fulfilment some five hundred years later.

"And Joshua charged them at that time, saying, Cursed before The LORD is the man who rises up and builds this city of Jericho. He shall lay the foundation of it in his first-born, and in his youngest son he shall set up the gates of it." (Joshua 6:26)

"In his days Hiel the man of Bethel built Jericho. He laid the foundation of it in Abiram his first-born, and set up the gates of it in his youngest son Segub, according to the Word of The LORD which He spoke by Joshua the son of Nun." 1 Kings 16:34

* Rebekah took the curse of Isaac. The result of this was so their son Jacob could receive his father's blessing in the place of his brother. Rebekah died as a consequence.

"And Jacob said to his mother Rebekah, Behold, Esau my brother is a hairy man, and I am a smooth man. My father will perhaps feel me, and I shall seem to him as a deceiver. And I shall bring a curse upon me, and not a blessing. And his mother said to him, Your curse be upon me, my son, only obey my voice and go bring them to me." Genesis 27:11

* And remember Matthew 27:24-25, where the Jews took the curse of the blood of Jesus on their own heads and those of the children. Within a generation some two million of them were murdered by the Romans, and then the survivors were finally driven out of their land in 70AD.

I've noticed that the power of word curses from others have greater impact when the person speaking them has authority such as a parent, pastor/priest, spouse or teacher. Our team have ministered with hundreds of people for whom this has been true. Some pastors have been known to proclaim *"If you ever leave this church you will be under a curse."* Former Roman Catholics have testified their parish priest said this frequently. Usually this is a control mechanism, but it still constitutes what Dr. Derek Prince called ***"Charismatic witchcraft."*** If that is ever said to anyone I am ministering to, I usually suggest they cut the curse off, shake the dust from their feet (as Jesus commanded) and get out of that church as quick as they can. Go and find a Christian fellowship that builds people up, edifies and equips them into fruitful discipleship in Jesus Christ

It is very clear that curses are powerful, and they impact very widely. The effects of a curse go on through a family line until someone knows how to stop them and acts to do so. That is the key purpose of this book.

Lastly, consider this vital verse:

"A city becomes great when the righteous give it their blessing; but a city is brought to ruin by the words of the wicked." Proverbs 11:11 (GNB)

I have a challenge for every one of us. Do you bless your city, or are you bringing about its ruin, by neglect? Are you blessing or cursing your community, city, or nation? When I was teaching on this in Zambia in Central Africa during late 2005, I sensed the Lord recommend that God's people should pray a blessing on their city and nation every morning as they said grace over their breakfast food. This word was well received, and I trust God will continue to take these words from an increasing number to truly bless that place. Why should your community miss out? What are you going to do about this? The next action should be yours. And tell others!

Chapter 3
Anti-Semitism & Racism

Christians need to remember that without Israel, we wouldn't have the Bible, or the Savior, or Forgiveness, or the Promises of Abraham. The Devil has always tried to kill the Jews because of this and because the Messiah also came from Israel.

When the Roman Emperor Constantine had a vision that resulted in his winning the Battle of Milvian Bridge, he later proclaimed freedom of religion for all in his empire. Instead of persecution, Christians were now a preferred people. Had it stopped there, things might have been successful, but Constantine had to "improve" Christianity. He brought in new "holy" days, replacing the Feasts of the LORD; he organized the Council of Nicea to develop a creed all were then made to adopt; he stamped his authority on Christianity and made it a religion with the requirement that saying words and doing rituals without a change of heart was sufficiently acceptable to the Emperor, but it failed to be acceptable to God.

Constantine changed the place of the Resurrection of Christ.
Constantine changed the time of the Resurrection of Christ.
Constantine changed the time of the birth of Christ.
Constantine changed the Scriptural method of becoming a Christian.
Constantine changed the relationship of Christianity to the state.
Constantine changed the headquarters from Jerusalem to Rome or Constantinople.

In time, the church became the Empire. The fundamental problem with that is that it totally misses the point of what Jesus stated.

"My kingdom is not of this world. If My kingdom were of this world, my servants would fight." John 18:36

So the claimed followers of Jesus began fighting to establish, defend and advance Christ's kingdom, something Jesus never told them to do. That's why we have a history of a church where Christians attack each other, fight religious wars, burn each other at the stake, mistake their earthly political kingdoms with the Kingdom of God, compromise the Gospel and their prophetic voice to gain political power.

Religious leaders from Constantine onwards were given state protection and preferences in many ways, including tax-free status. The position of bishops went for sale to the highest bidder, popes became political manipulators who were notoriously immoral, dissent was met with brutal force, the poor were oppressed and exploited, people were killed for translating the Bible into the languages of the common people.

In effect, the church became the same as the leaders of Israel during Jesus' time, the Pharisees, Sadducees and Scribes, who would do anything to keep the power they had over the people, including kill the man who had clearly proven Himself to be the Messiah. The bottom line is this: When the Christians focus on earthly political power, both the Christians and the world lose. Instead of preaching and living the Gospel, showing the love of Jesus, speaking prophetic truth to the culture, healing the sick and raising the dead (both spiritually and physically), Christian fight each other, compromise, manipulate, back-stab, and present an awful witness to the world. The world loses a vital Gospel witness it so desperately needs, and the church loses it's spiritual power.

I believe it's time to stop compromising with the world and the emperor/caesar! We are called to obey our true King. It's time to stop choosing between the lesser of two evils when both are evil. Let His light shine through us. *(This has been covered in some depth in my book, "Rediscovering a Biblical Faith.")* Constantine pronounced many curses against all the Jewish people and their obedience to the commands of God, as seen in the following curse.

The Curse of Constantine

"I renounce all customs, rites, legalisms, unleavened breads and sacrifices of lambs of the Hebrews, and all the other feasts of the Hebrews, sacrifices, prayers, aspirations, purifications, sanctifications, and propitiations, and fasts and new moons, and Sabbaths, and superstitions, and hymns and chants, and observances and synagogues, absolutely everything Jewish, every law, rite and customs and if afterwards I shall wish to deny and return to Jewish superstition or shall be found eating with Jews, or feasting with them, or secretly conversing and condemning the Christian religion instead of openly confuting them and condemning their vain faith, then let the trembling of Cain and the leprosy of Gehazi cleave to me, as well as the legal punishments to which I acknowledge myself liable. And may I be an anathema (curse) in the world to come, and may my soul be set down with the Satan and the devils."

Bible scholars such as Dr. Derek Prince have identified anti-Semitism as the root of all racism. The pigment or color of your skin is irrelevant to your character, your faith or your integrity.

> **"And The LORD said to Abram, Go out of your country, and from your kindred, and from your father's house into a land that I will show you. And I will make you a great nation. And I will bless you and make your name great. And you shall be a blessing. And I will bless those that bless you and curse the one who curses you. And in you shall all families of the earth be blessed." (Genesis 12:1-3)**

It seems clear that God has strong feelings about the children of Abraham and people's attitudes to them. How does this affect Gentile Christians?

> **"Therefore know that those of faith, these are the sons of Abraham. And the Scripture, foreseeing that God would justify the nations through faith, preached the gospel before to Abraham, saying, "In you shall all nations be blessed." So then those of faith are blessed with faithful Abraham. For as many as are out of works of the Law, these are under a curse; for it is written, "Cursed is everyone who does not continue in all things which are written in the Book of the Law, to do them." But that no one is justified by the Law in the sight of God is clear, for, "The just shall live by faith." But the Law is not of faith; but, "The man who does these things shall live in them." Christ redeemed us from the curse of the Law,**

being made a curse for us (for it is written, "Cursed is everyone having been hanged on a tree"); so that the blessing of Abraham might be to the nations in Jesus Christ, and that we might receive the promise of the Spirit through faith." Galatians 3:7-14

We do remember the curse the Jews at the time of Pilate during the judgement of Jesus (Matthew 27:24-25) where they stated in clear terms that His blood should be on their heads and those of their children. If they had known then the terrible curse they spoke over themselves and their family lines, I wonder if their words might have been different. Pilate killed hundreds of thousands of Jews in the decade following Calvary, and within a generation the Jews were expelled from their homeland by Roman/Syrian General Titus in 70AD. For over 1800 years Jews were forbidden to live in the land God had promised they should have.

By 100 AD the early church was removing many of the Feasts of the LORD and other elements of the Book of Acts faith. Part of the problem is that the institutional church has historically been anti-Semitic, so all Christians are affected to some measure because of this history.

Constantine instructed the removal of much more "Jewish" influence from the church and its life and practise. He wanted to divorce Rome's empire from Judaism, and he largely succeeded. This opened the door for further error to come in. Writing of the Easter Observance, Dr. Henry Percival quotes, *"It was declared to be particularly unworthy for this, the holiest of festivals to following the customs of the Jews who had soiled their hands with the most fearful of crimes and whose minds were blinded... We ought not therefore to have anything in common with the Jew, for the Savior has shown us another way... we desire, dearest brethren, to separate ourselves from the detestable company of the Jew."* ("The Nicean and Post-Nicean Fathers", by Dr. Henry R. Percival Vol. xiv, Edmans, Grand Rapids 1979 pps 54-55)

The institutional church began to teach that Jews were enemies of God, and St. Augustine continued this line. *"Furthermore the Church Fathers taught that the unfaithfulness of the Jewish people resulted in a collective guilt which made them subject to the permanent curse of God,"* according to Marvin Wilson. ("Our Father Abraham.")

"Martin Luther was greatly used by God in the 16th century to restore the church from the Dark Ages... to the original truth of salvation by grace through faith. At the beginning he tried to win the Jews to the Lord, as he understood that they were still the people of God and that the Gentile Christians had alienated them. However the Jews had suffered several crusades and the Spanish Inquisition. They totally rejected Luther's attempts to win them to the Gospel.

Due to that, Luther became bitter and developed a vehement hatred against the Jews. He issued a series of articles and pamphlets, including "On the Jews and their Lies." In those he labelled Jews as "venomous," "thieves," and "disgusting vermin." The seed of hatred and anti-Semitism was transmitted through Luther to all Protestant Christians," according to Dominiquae Bierman. (The Healing Power of the Roots" 1996.)

Luther also said that Jews were only fit to be slaves of slaves, and that it was good if they could be burned to death in their synagogues. German Nazi dictator Adolf Hitler found in Luther's writings a wealth of support for his evil plan to exterminate all Jews from the face of the earth: "The Final Solution." The resulting holocaust appals many people to this day, although not those under the spell of anti-Semitism or the principalities and powers that empower this.

There is another branch of anti-Semitism: it is called "Replacement Theology." This teaching claims that the Christian church has replaced Israel in God's plan for the end times. This is a false teaching and a heresy. Those who push this mistaken and erroneous belief have to ignore the clear statements from Scriptures mentioned above, and others. It is obvious proponents then come under the curse God proclaims on those who oppose His plans and purposes for the people of Israel. At it's root, Replacement Theology is racism. There are many other Scriptures that support what I am saying, and too much of the Bible must be ignored in order to accommodate such a false belief as Replacement Theology.

Whether we like it or not, God has a special plan and purpose for the people of Israel, often called "the Jews." They are imperfect, they can be difficult, cantankerous, and every group of ten of them will have at least eleven opinions. But God has chosen them for Himself, in part as a lesson for the rest of humankind. The sooner we wake up to this truth, the sooner we will understand more of God's end-time plans. Christians were grafted into Israel, not the other way around. The people of Israel are waking up as there are more Jewish Believers that Yeshua/Jesus is the Messiah today than have lived in almost 2000 years.

Israel has paid a terrible price for the curse of 30 A.D. Today, during our lifetimes, Israel is being grafted back into God's purposes. We are witnesses to the miracle of a nation reborn after 1900 years. This is unprecedented.

In John chapter 17, Jesus prayed for the unity of His disciples. He went further and stated that our love and unity would be a sign that we are, indeed, His disciples. I am not alone in believing that division by our denominations is a sure sign of a curse on the church due to the historic anti-Semitism. There is one God, one Father, One Son, one Holy Spirit, and only one Body of Christ. I believe it is time for the ecclesia/church to rise up and put an end to human and demonic division and to come into divine unity so we can welcome our Bridegroom when He returns for us. *(There is a suitable prayer for this on page 97.)*

A Biblical Curse - and Arab Muslim Degradation

We read the famous promise from God, **"I will bless those who bless you and curse him who curses you,"** (Genesis 12:3, [JPS translation]).

In many ways, Biblical Hebrew is more sensitive than English. For example, in an English text, the word, 'curse' in this is repeated: God says, **"he who curses you I will curse."** But in the Hebrew text, two different words are used. The 'curse' that others place upon Israel is the word, *"m'kalellchah"* - and the curse that God will use is *'ah-or'* (pardon my transliteration).

Consider the difference between *'m'kahlellchah'* and *'ah-or.'* That difference tells us a lot about the Arab Muslims who incite to kill Jews today - and the self-imposed degradation that so frustrates them.

The Jewish commentary known at the Klei Yakar [Rabbi Shlomo Ephraim ben Aaron Luntschitz (1550-1619)], explains the meaning of these two words. He begins by translating the curse against Israel, called *'M'kalellchah.'* This word, he says, contains a meaning that combines concepts of blasphemy, scorn and contempt, [Kli Yakar, Breisheet, volume 1, Menucha publications, Brooklyn, NY, 2013, p 170; translation by Elihu Levine].

'Blasphemy' contains these elements: showing a heightened disrespect to God and to that which is Holy, and acts that insult and/or disrespect God.

'Scorn' contains several elements: harsh criticism that shows a lack of respect, rejection, derision, refusal to acknowledge, treating someone as despicable.

'Contempt' contains these elements: a wilful, open disrespect of law, treating someone (or the law) as if they (or it) is not worthy of any respect whatsoever.

Arab Muslims blaspheme against the God of Israel. They don't just disrespect Jewish Holy sites. They spit at them. They firebomb them. They tear them down when they can.

Arab Muslims scorn all things Jewish. They call Jews apes and pigs. They deny any Jewish connection to the land of Israel. They mock their Jewish victims. Arab Muslims have such contempt for law they have declared that killing Jews is legal. Instead of condemning the murder of Jews, they glorify it. They legitimize violence. Their Islamic clergy says Jews are not worthy to live. Arab Muslims curse Jews with blasphemy, scorn and contempt. But as the Bible says, those who curse Jews with *'m'kalellchah'* are themselves cursed with *'ah-or.'*

The Klei Yakar translates *'ah-or'* as *'a grievous curse.'* This type of curse, he explains, contains elements best described as 'degradation.'

'Degradation' suggests a process that leads to destruction. It suggests a condition of damage and ruin.

For example, look at Gaza. In 2005, Israel voluntarily made Gaza Jew-free. With a single - and singular - Jewish decision, Gazans had the opportunity to do anything they wanted. The Jews were gone. Some said Gaza would now become the Singapore of the Middle East.

That didn't happen. These Arab Muslims who so viciously cursed Jews chose Hamas. They didn't get economic development. They got ruin.

The Palestinian Authority is only slightly better. Those people on the so-called "West Bank" chose Abbas. They didn't get economic cooperation with Israel. They got incitement to kill Jews - along with political oppression, corruption and economic stagnation.

Israel is not the cause of this state of degradation. This degradation is Arab Muslim-made. Because Arabs choose curses over blessings, they reject cooperation with Israel. That rejection is suicidal.

The physical environment of the Middle East is harsh. Israel has shown it has the know-how to thrive in such a harsh place. To reject that know-how is the fast-track to ruin. Arabs have brought this ruin upon themselves. They're schizophrenic: Arab Muslims in Gaza and the West Bank say they want more economic cooperation with Israel. But they also say they want to see Israel destroyed. For these Arab Muslims, economic cooperation with Israel would be good. But destroying Israel is better. Therefore, they choose politicians and Islamic clergy who promote the latter over the former.

Because of those leaders, they curse the Jews. They end up cursed. The Bible is correct. Don't curse what God loves. You can't win.

The Curse of Ham

Most people know about Noah and his flood. Fewer seem to know of the trouble that followed after the family and animals reached dry land. The Curse of Ham refers to the supposed curse upon Canaan, Ham's son, that was imposed by the Biblical patriarch Noah. The curse occurs in the Book of Genesis and concerns Noah's drunkenness and the accompanying shameful act perpetrated by his son Ham, the father of Canaan, (Genesis 9:20–27). The controversies raised by this story regarding the nature of Ham's transgression, and the question of why Noah cursed Canaan when Ham had sinned, have been debated for over 2,000 years. This has been used to explain falsely why the descendents of Ham (mostly Africans and African-Americans, etc.) should be subjected to slavery and poverty

Other ancient commentators suggested that Ham was guilty of more than what the Bible says. The Targum Onqelos has Ham gossiping about his father's drunken disgrace *"in the street"* (a reading that has a basis in the original Hebrew), so that being held up to public mockery was what had angered Noah; as the Cave of Treasures (4th century) puts it, **"Ham laughed at his father's shame and did not cover it, but laughed about it and mocked."**

Ancient commentaries have also debated whether "seeing" someone's nakedness meant to have sex with that person, (e.g. Leviticus 20:17). The same idea was raised by 3rd-century rabbis, in the Babylonian Talmud (c. 500 AD), who argue that Ham either castrated his father, or sodomised him. The same explanations are found in three Greek translations of the Bible, that replace the word "see" in verse 22 with another word denoting homosexual relations. The castration theory has its modern counterpart in suggested parallels found in the castration of Uranus by Cronus in Greek mythology and a Hittite myth of the supreme god Anu whose genitals were *"bitten off by his rebel son and cup-bearer Kumarbi, who afterwards rejoiced and laughed ... until Anu cursed him."*

The Bible says that Canaan, Ham's son, was cursed, not Ham himself. Thus, only one of Ham's four sons, not all four, were cursed. How then could all black people everywhere be cursed? The Bible places limitations on curses - only three or four generations at most,(Exodus 20:5). The curse on Canaan and his descendants, **"Now there, you are cursed, and none of you shall be freed from being slaves,"** finds its most obvious fulfillment in the ongoing defeat and subjugation of Canaan by Israel, (Joshua 9:23; 1 Kings 9:20-21). The descendants of Ham's other sons - Cush, Mizraim, and Put-have continued to this day as national peoples in Ethiopia (Cush), Egypt (Mizraim), and Libya (Put).

God says that curses based on disobedience are reversed when people repent and turn again to obedience, (Exodus 20:6). This is certainly sufficient to cancel the enslavement of Africans. The apostle Paul told masters to treat converted slaves as equal brothers in Christ, (Philemon 1:15-16). They forgot that the apostle Paul said that slaves had the right to try to change their status, (1 Corinthians 7:21). And they forgot that the masters' authority over slaves was limited. It was not within the master's rights to treat a slave in an inhumane manner. Masters were to apply the Golden Rule to slaves and were not to treat them as children of a lesser god. The God who rules both heaven and earth will show no partiality to those who commit evil against humankind, whether slave or free.

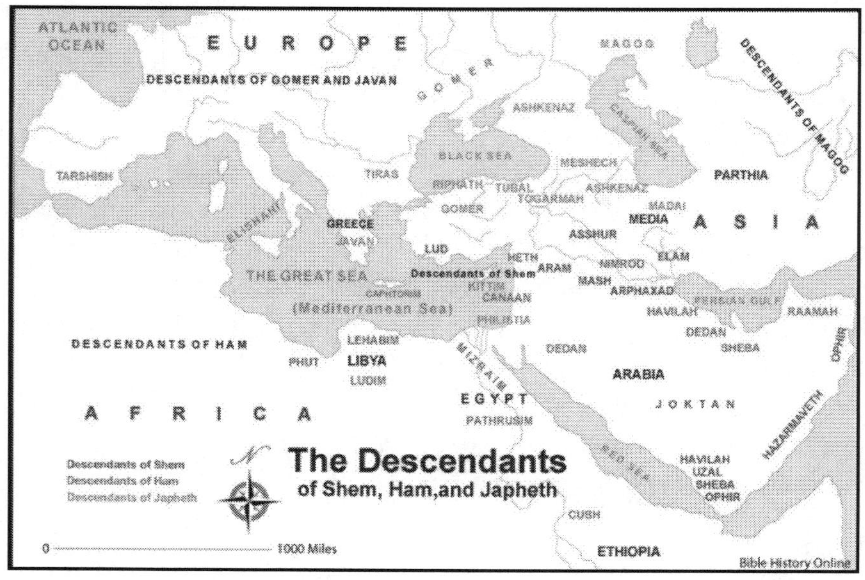

Chapter 4
Unforgiveness

Forgiveness means ripping up the I.O.U.'s. We must forgive because Jesus has forgiven us.

Forgiveness is commanded by God and is something we do in obedience to God. Forgiveness is a decision of our will - we can choose to forgive!

"For if you forgive men their trespasses, your heavenly Father will also forgive you. But if you do not forgive men their trespasses, neither will your Father forgive your trespasses." Matthew 6:14-15

"Therefore, as the elect of God, holy and beloved, put on tender mercies, kindness, humility, meekness, long-suffering; bearing with one another, and forgiving one another, if anyone has a complaint against another; even as Christ forgave you, so you also must do." Colossians 3:12-13

These scriptures raise an interesting point. If God chooses to forgive us to the measure we forgive others, any failure on our part to forgive someone else could be understood to mean that God will also withhold His forgiveness. Any failure to forgive by us then becomes a salvation issue, if these words of Jesus mean what a dictionary states.

The Lord's Prayer

"So, then, you should pray this way: Our Father who is in Heaven, Hallowed be Your name. Your kingdom come; Your will be done, as it is in Heaven, also on the earth. Give us today our daily bread, and forgive us our debts as we also forgive our debtors. And do not lead us into temptation, but deliver us from the evil one, for Yours is the kingdom and the power and the glory to the ages. Amen. For if you forgive men their trespasses, your heavenly Father will also forgive you." Matthew 6:9-14

Please note verse 12 - **"forgive us our debts as we also forgive our debtors."** We each have a choice to make, and in making it there will be consequences.

Many (some say "most") emotional and psychological/psychiatric problems could be resolved if only people would forgive. Many people who suffer from depression have issues of unforgiveness to deal with prior to their depression lifting. (I've confirmed that with several psychiatrists I've spoken with in a number of nations.) We need to understand that harboring unforgiveness will open your soul to demonic torment, (Matthew 18:34); and that for forgiveness to be genuine it must touch the heart and emotions and be released to God. Jesus teaches us the following:

> **"Then Peter came to Him and said, "Lord, how often shall my brother sin against me, and I forgive him? Up to seven times?" Jesus said to him, "I do not say to you, up to seven times, but up to seventy times seven. So My heavenly Father also will do to you if each of you, from his heart, does not forgive his brother his trespasses." Matthew 18:21-22, 35**

1. Forgiveness does not mean tolerating abuse

> **"If it is possible, as much as depends on you, live peaceably with all men. Beloved, do not avenge yourselves, but rather give place to wrath; for it is written, "Vengeance is Mine, I will repay," says the Lord. Therefore If your enemy is hungry, feed him; if he is thirsty, give him a drink; for in so doing you will heap coals of fire on his head. Do not be overcome by evil, but overcome evil with good." Romans 12:18-21**

2. Forgiveness does not mean you approve of the person's behavior

> **"But I say to you who hear: Love your enemies, do good to those who hate you, bless those who curse you, and pray for those who spitefully use you." Luke 6:27-28**

3. Forgiveness is a decision of the will to release the person who has wronged you of any debt or commitment or apology that you feel they owe you and to release all bitterness to God

> **"Pursue peace with all people, and holiness, without which no one will see the Lord: looking diligently lest anyone fall short of the grace of God; lest any root of bitterness springing up cause trouble, and by this many become defiled;" Hebrews 12:14-15**

> **"Let all bitterness, wrath, anger, clamour, and evil speaking be put away from you, with all malice. And be kind to one another, tenderhearted, forgiving one another, just as God in Christ forgave you." Ephesians 4:31-32**

4. If you have unforgiveness toward someone, you will begin to react emotionally every time you are around that person. If you do not forgive someone, you are allowing that person to control you!

> **"Now the Lord is the Spirit; and where the Spirit of the Lord is, there is liberty." 2 Corinthians 3:17**

When you do not forgive someone who has hurt you, you aren't ruling your own spirit or will, and you will leave yourself wide open to attack from the enemy.

> **"Whoever has no rule over his own spirit is like a city broken down, without walls." Proverbs 25:28**

The Devil is the accuser of the brethren and he delights in inflicting condemning thoughts in your head. If you have truly forgiven those that have hurt you, it takes away his control over that part of your life. Your heart will be joyous that you have already taken care of that unforgiveness and it will make you stronger and not ashamed in the sight of God.

"Be sober, be vigilant; because your adversary the devil walks about like a roaring lion, seeking whom he may devour." 1 Peter 5:8

There will be a time when the devil will no longer be able to accuse us.

"Then I heard a loud voice saying in heaven, "Now salvation, and strength, and the kingdom of our God, and the power of His Christ have come, for the accuser of our brethren, who accused them before our God day and night, has been cast down." Revelation 12:10

Until that time we must be on our guard to prevent him from getting a foot-hold in our lives.

Seven Steps to Forgiving Others

"The first step is for you to choose to forgive that person for the specific offences against you.

The second step is to ask God to forgive that person. Earnestly ask that He will no longer hold anything against that person on your account.

The third step is to ask God to forgive you for holding unforgiveness, resentment, anger, bitterness or even hatred in your heart.

In the fourth step you forgive God for allowing this person to hurt you. You may think God doe not need to be forgiven. Indeed He doesn't, but you need the exercise in forgiving Him.

*Ventilation of stored-up emotions is **the crucial fifth step**. Anger turned inward is a common reason for depression. Feel free to cry, sob, hit a pillow, (but not the cat or dog), go for a brisk walk - especially in the rain if possible or other strenuous exercise can be most helpful to get rid of bitterness and frustration.*

The sixth step is a request for God to pour His healing balm over your wounds and painful memories and to let Him fill you with His love and presence.

__The seventh step__ is directed towards the offender. You ask God to bless him or her in every way possible, spiritually, physically, socially financially, at home, at work, in every aspect of life."
(Doris Boydston, Mental Health Unit Supervisor, Palmdale General Hospital, California; Article "How to Walk Free")

I was asked by a pastor to pray with a 60 years old woman who had severe arthritis was aided by a walking frame, and was scheduled to have operations on her knees and ankles in two weeks. As usual I asked Holy Spirit what the key was and He said "Unforgiveness." I asked the woman if there was there anyone she should forgive, and she replied, *"That will be my Ex!"* I then led her through a short prayer forgiving, and then blessed her Ex. Almost immediately she ended up on the ground. My prayer partner and I both discerned a spirit had knocked her over. We evicted the spirit and kept praying. In less than two minutes, the woman got up, folded her walking frame under her arm and left to cancel the operations.

In that same church, the senior pastor asked me to pray with a particular group of twenty people, while others in the ministry team I had been training dealt with other folks. I asked what was unique about this group, and was told they were the patients from the Psych unit of the local hospital. The first in the queue was a very attractive woman in her early twenties. Again I asked Holy Spirit what the key was, and again He said "Unforgiveness." I introduced myself and asked her name, which she told me without looking at me. A man stepped forward beside her and said he was a new pastor and this young woman was one of his congregation. I asked the young woman if there was anyone she should forgive. She replied, *"I have to, to be free, don't I?"* I replied I believed so. With a very quiet voice, and still looking at the carpet, she then named a man. I explained briefly it would be helpful to forgive and then bless that man in all things relevant to his life, his health, work, relationships, etc. Through the fog of her medication, I then led her through a brief prayer, with her pastor also participating. By the time we finished a couple of minutes later, this young woman was looking me full in the face and had a huge smile. God had done something significant. She went back to the hospital to collect her things, and under her doctor's supervision, was off all her medication within two weeks. A year later she was happily married.

Her pastor was so grateful he invited me to come to his town and train his congregation too.

This topic of forgiveness is not theory, but crucial for freedom for many.

How to Deal with Unforgiveness

We ask for the Holy Spirit to bring to our mind the name of every person that we have any unforgiveness or bitterness toward. We should write down these names (or initials if preferred). This list does not have to be shared with anyone, but each one needs to be dealt with as the Lord shows you.

Should you be doing personal ministry with someone who needs to forgive, you may find it helpful to pray for the Holy Spirit to enable them to release unforgiveness from their heart for each person on their list, being careful not to omit putting their own name on the list as we often have the hardest problem forgiving ourselves.

The person should pray through their list one person at a time, forgiving each person from their heart; not forgetting to ask God for forgiveness for blaming Him and also asking that all bitterness against Him be released. This is very important because if bitterness toward God is not released, future spiritual growth will be thwarted.

Close the session in prayer asking God to protect and seal the work that the Lord and you have done.

Ask the person if there is anything that is not on this list they feel should be added.

> **"And be kind to one another, tenderhearted, forgiving one another, even as God for Christ's sake has forgiven you." Ephesians 4:32**

Nothing Can Replace Forgiveness

"You can repent of your sins until you are hoarse, confess your faith to all, pray without ceasing, give everything you have to the work of

God, read the Bible everyday and still block God's forgiveness by an unforgiving heart. No amount of repenting, confessing, prayer or reading the Word will ever cover over, atone for, or excuse unforgiveness! There is nothing you can do that can take the place of forgiveness:

Forgiveness is NOT tolerance;
Forgiveness is NOT pretending;
Forgiveness is NOT forgetting;
Forgiveness is NOT generosity of spirit;
Forgiveness is NOT turning the other cheek;
Forgiveness is NOT looking the other way;
Forgiveness is NOT making a joke of wrong;
Forgiveness is NOT politeness or tactfulness;
Forgiveness is NOT diplomacy;
Forgiveness is NOT a passive non-response.
Forgiveness is something much deeper.
Forgiveness IS a deliberate act of the will;
Forgiveness IS a full pardon;
Forgiveness IS a substitutional act;
Forgiveness IS obedience to God's Word;
Forgiveness IS an act of love;
Forgiveness IS the key to Freedom."

("Shattering Your Strongholds", © Liberty Savard, p 101.)

Freedom from guilt and condemnation are God's response when we deal with this issue with a humble heart.

Let us summarize this:
    Forgiveness does not mean tolerating abuse
    Does not mean you approve of the person's behavior
    Forgiveness is a decision of the will
    Forgiveness is commanded by God and is something we do in obedience to Him.

Chapter 5
Idolatry & Witchcraft

On 1 January 1804, a former slave, Jean-Jaqcues Dessalines, declared the freedom of St. Domingues and founded the first Black Empire in the world, Haiti. How did he do it? Through the Bois Caïman ceremony of August 1791. This voodoo ceremony began the Haitian Revolution. During the ceremony, the dark-skinned and scarred warrior-mother, Ezili Dantor, the patron goddess of women and children, possessed a priestess. A black pig was offered to her since she has a weakness for black pigs. All present pledged to fight for freedom from slavery and oppression. This ceremony ultimately resulted in the "liberation" of the Haitian people from French colonial rule, which they swapped for occultism and continuing poverty.

God forbids us from having any other gods, making images of them or worshipping them. He says in His Word that He is jealous, and that He will not share His glory with anyone or anything else.

> **"You shall have no other gods before Me. You shall not make to yourselves any graven image, or any likeness of anything that is in the heavens above, or that is in the earth beneath, or that is in the water under the earth. You shall not bow yourself down to them, nor serve them. For I The LORD your God am a jealous God, visiting the iniquity of the fathers upon the sons to the third and fourth generation of those that hate me," Exodus 20:3-5**

God repeats this stern instruction elsewhere, including:

> **"Cursed is the man that makes any graven or molten image, an abomination to The LORD, the work of the hands of the craftsman, and puts it in a secret place. And all the people shall answer and say, Amen." Deuteronomy 27:15**

In every Biblical list of things that will keep people out of God's heaven, idolatry, witchcraft and other occultic activities are clearly among the key items included.

"Now the works of the flesh are clearly revealed, which are: adultery, fornication, uncleanness, lustfulness, idolatry, sorcery, hatreds, fightings, jealousies, angers, rivalries, divisions, heresies, envyings, murders, drunkennesses, revelings, and things like these; of which I tell you before, as I also said before, that they who do such things shall not inherit the kingdom of God." Galatians 5:19-21

"There shall not be found among you anyone who makes his son or his daughter to pass through the fire, or that uses divination, an observer of clouds, or a fortune-teller, or a witch, or a charmer, or a consulter with familiar spirits, or a wizard, or one who calls to the dead. For all that do these things are an abomination to The LORD. And because of these abominations The LORD your God drives them out from before you." Deuteronomy 18:10-12

"And the rest of the men who were not killed by these plagues still did not repent of the works of their hands, that they should not worship demons, and golden, and silver, and bronze, and stone, and wooden idols (which neither can see, nor hear, nor walk)." Revelation 9:20

Let's have a look at a scripture, that has a different angle on this issue.

"I am The LORD, and there is none else, no God besides Me; I clothed you, though you have not known Me;" Isaiah 45:5

It is very clear that no other being that pretends to deity will be tolerated by the one true God. He isn't going to allow us to have Allah, or Buddha, or even Mary alongside Him. Mary was an honorable young teenager when she was chosen by God with the special task of giving birth to the Savior of the world. But she was subject to the iniquities of her ancestors. (It's a medical fact that every human baby's blood never crosses with it's mother's. That's why we have paternity tests to determine fathers.) She also made offering for her sins following the birth of Jesus recorded in Luke 2. The issue is that no one other then

Jesus died for our sins, and consequently we need to get our beliefs and thinking back in line with God's word. Any other teaching that is inconsistent with God's word is wrong, no matter the status of those who have taught it.

I am concerned at the veneration of Mary that borders on worship. Let us not forget Mary's last recorded words in Scripture at the time of the wedding at Cana. She said, **"This is my son, listen to him and do what he says,"** John 2:5. Mary never sought importance or any position of influence for herself, contrary to the teachings of some.

Related to this issue is the crucifix. That is a cross with the body of Jesus still nailed to it. This is a symbol of a dead, defeated and powerless Jesus. In his own eyes this is Satan's biggest victory. The death of Jesus fulfilled God's plan, and so did the fact that He rose from the dead and is no longer powerless. We need a living Lord Jesus to save and assist us.

Have you noticed that in countries ruled by dictators, such as Saddam Hussein of Iraq, or Kim Jong Un of North Korea, not forgetting the Soviet Union and Cuba. Their leader's image is everywhere, in paintings and photos. Its purpose is to keep their people in subjugation. **The leader is watching you**. In the same way the crucifix has been used to keep millions of people under the bondage of religion for the last several centuries. Anything that displeases God should be rejected. A crucifix is certainly an idol to millions of Roman Catholics and Orthodox followers whose church leaders have brought the people under a curse because of this practice. While I didn't enjoy the research, to help set people free from curses of all forms, I wrote *"Rome's Anathemas: Insights into the papal Pantheon."* A prayer for all former Roman Catholics is available in that book, and the E-book on our website. The word "Anathema" means "Curse" in Greek.

False gods do have power - they are empowered by principalities, powers and rulers of darkness, according to Scripture. Besides, when we consider what God's word says about idols and false gods, we would be foolish, even spiritually blinded, to participate in such an activity or belief.

> **"Their idols are silver and gold, the work of men's hands. They have mouths, but they do not speak; they have eyes, but they do not see; they have ears, but they do not hear; they have noses, but they do not smell; they have hands, but they do not handle; they have feet, but they do not walk; they do not mutter through their throat. The ones who make them are like them, and everyone who trusts in them." Psalm 115:4-8**

Let me make this very clear. Any prayer offered through anyone but Jesus Christ is idolatry. We cannot serve the God of Abraham and Isaac and Jacob on the weekends, and then talk to any of these others, including his mother, during the week.

I have noticed that where idolatry is common, there is violence, poverty, drugs, and dictatorship by government. The issue is about curses that prevent God's people from coming in to the fullness of God's promises. He gives us the choice having outlined the issues.

> **"Behold! I have set before you today life and good, and death and evil," Deuteronomy 30:15**

God has given us a very clear choice.

There is another issue here - that of Generational involvement in the occult, including covens and organizations such as Freemasonry and other similar Secret Societies. Our ministry teams - and many others we have trained all around the world - have helped tens of thousands break free from the bondages of such family involvements. Because of Iniquities mentioned in Genesis 20:5 and other verses, family involvement in these practices has brought untold emotional, physical and spiritual misery and suffering to millions. Space prevents them being covered again here. I recommend you obtain whichever book may best suit your family's involvements from the following: "Unmasking Freemasonry," "Unmasking Mormonism," "Unmasking the Watchtower," "Unmasking Spiritualism," "The New Age - Old Lie in a New Package." *(Details on how to obtain these resources may be found on the last pages.)*

Chapter 6
Sexual Abuse & Perversion

Let us check out a comprehensive list in **Leviticus 18:1-30** that God states very clearly that Adultery, Incest, Fornication, Homosexuality and Bestiality are practices He will judge severely. God then goes on to say what will happen if anyone does those things He calls abominable:

"Do not defile yourselves in any of these things. For in all these the nations are defiled, which I cast out before you. And the land is defiled. Therefore I visit its wickedness on it, and the land itself vomits out those who live in it. You shall therefore keep My statutes and My judgments, and shall not commit any of these abominations, neither the native, nor any stranger that lives among you. For the men of the land who were before you have done all these abominations, and the land is defiled. You shall not do these so that the land may not spew you out also when you defile it, as it spewed out the nations that were before you. For whoever shall commit any of these abominations, even the souls who commit them shall be cut off from among their people. And you shall keep My ordinance, so as not to do any of these abominable customs which were committed before you, and that you do not defile yourselves in them. I am The LORD your God." Leviticus 18:24-30

Adultery is sex with anyone you aren't married to, when you are married. Incest is sex with a family member other than your covenant marriage partner. Fornication is sex with anyone prior to marriage. Homosexuality is sex with a member of the same sex or gender. Bestiality is sex with an animal. ***All are cursed by God, full stop!***

Practising them (along with the other things listed) will keep any person out of God's Kingdom, according to Galatians 5:21.

"Whoever commits adultery with a woman lacks understanding; he who does it destroys his own soul." Proverbs 6:32

That seems very clear too, whether we like it or not. If you have ever participated in any of these activities, then you are under a curse from God.

The solution is easy. Repent, ask His forgiveness and cleansing and don't do it again. God's mercy will then extend to you in a fresh and cleansing way.

God's ways are the right ways and they bring blessing to those who choose them. Hiding these and all others sins doesn't work in the long run, as it states in:

"You will never succeed in life if you try to hide your sins. Confess them and give them up; then God will show mercy to you." Proverbs 28:13 (GNB)

Chapter 7 - Hurting Helpless People

God wants us all to look after those who are vulnerable due to circumstances beyond their control. This is one of the more comprehensive lists:

"Cursed is the man that makes any graven or moulten image, an abomination to The LORD, the work of the hands of the craftsman, and puts it in a secret place. And all the people shall answer and say, Amen. Cursed is he who thinks lightly of his father or his mother. And all the people shall say, Amen. Cursed is he who removes his neighbor's landmark. And all the people shall say, Amen. Cursed is he who makes the blind to wander out of the way. And all the people shall say, Amen. Cursed is he who perverts the judgment of the stranger, fatherless, and widow. And all the people shall say, Amen.

Cursed is he who strikes his neighbor secretly. And all the people shall say, Amen. Cursed is he who takes reward to kill an innocent person. And all the people shall say, Amen. Cursed is he who does not confirm all the words of this Law, to do them. And all the people shall say, Amen." Deuteronomy 27:15-19, 24-26

Some of this relates to and duplicates the issues of inappropriate sexual activity as covered in the previous chapter. Those issues are repeated here because they involve taking advantage of the innocent, or those that could be easily abused. Notice that God states **"Cursed is"** with every issue He raises in this passage. We need to take this seriously. God does! The people's responses with each statement makes them subject to the curse of a rash vow if they ever broke their promise over these issues.

There are other issues of taking advantage over others - as the following shows:

"Come now, rich ones, weep and howl for your hardships coming on. Your riches have rotted, and your clothes have become moth-eaten. Your gold and silver have corroded, and their poison will be a witness against you, and will eat your flesh as fire. You heaped treasure in the last days. Behold, the hire of the labourers reaping your fields cry out, being kept back by you. And the cries of those who have reaped have entered into the ears of the Lord of hosts. You have lived luxuriously on the earth, and lived wantonly. You have nourished your hearts, as in a day of slaughter." James 5:1-5

This is also showing that slavery and abuse of wage-earners who work for you isn't acceptable to God. If you employ people to do work, then please pay them a fair rate, and don't quibble, or be dishonest or stingy, or you could end up under a curse of God, according to His Word.

"I will come near to you for judgement. I will be quick to testify against sorcerers, adulterers and perjurers, against those who defraud labourers of their wages, who oppress the widows and the fatherless, and deprive aliens of justice, but do not fear me, says the LORD Almighty." Malachi 3:5 (NIV)

Israel was in the bondage of slavery for 400 years, but they left with much of the wealth of Egypt. That was 400 years of back pay, so God has a way of putting things right.

Arrested Development Issues

Science and medicine don't seem to be able to repair people very well who suffer from this range of problems. The main reason why is that these are spiritual in nature, and science doesn't understand that. Humans are triune beings, created by God with a spirit, a soul and a body. A learning disability has been defined as *"a disorder in which an individual's brain handles information in a way that blocks learning."*

The arresting process usually begins in childhood and shows up by school age, if not earlier. Experience is gained by learning, with the accumulation of knowledge, and understanding resulting in growing maturity. It's how we learn to read and write, to do maths, and develop social skills to cope with teen years and adulthood as we get older.

For example, our cognitive skills that can be impaired are: Oral expressions, Listening comprehension, Written expression, Basic reading skills, Reading comprehension, Maths calculation, Mathematical reasoning ability and Spelling ability. Those who have problems with the three "R's" will also usually have difficulties with motion, spatial relationships, memory, communication, impulsiveness and attention spans. As implied above, the secular world do have some skills to help improve many of these situations, but because of the spiritual dynamic, 100% healing is virtually impossible without attending to the spiritual realm.

We are all well aware of neurological issues, some caused by brain damage, others by outright neglect. Babies should receive the right interaction and stimulation by parents, and if that doesn't occur within the first two years, it can be very difficult to make up for lost time. There are known cases where Downs Syndrome children have been basically abandoned in their cot, causing huge developmental delays.

In addition, anyone doing ministry and/or counseling will have come across people who suffered a major trauma, resulting in Dissociation. Again, this is primarily a spiritual issue, where the person's soul splits, and a part stays the same age as when the trauma occurs. If the trauma is on-going sexual abuse, there will be multiple soul-parts at each of the ages these occurred. It's been well documented that people get stuck at that emotional age, which prevents the person from learning, changing and growing. This may be a significant reason some children can't learn at school, because they are stuck at an emotionally immature age much less than their biological age. Examples can include being afraid to start something in case they fail, or they are emotionally overwhelmed so they avoid attempting anything of value, and experience frustration, low self-esteem or hopelessness, and probably all of the above. Powerlessness freezes the will and the mind so you can't do anything to help yourself. Hopelessness makes you believe it isn't worth trying.

Both biological and spiritual parents should learn to provide true empowerment teaching from a young age, getting children to believe in themselves, learning perseverance when things get difficult, and celebrating achievements, regardless of how significant these might be.

Humanity's main spiritual opponent, the devil, knows that if growth in any one of these three areas can be stunted, it will weaken the entire person, and probably bring the death of genuine expectations for that person, meaning they'll never achieve their full potential.

Arrested Development causes perpetual babyhood. What are required are teachers and counselors who can teach the First Principals of the Bible (Hebrews 5:12-14; 6:1-2).

The spirits that cause Arrested Development work closely with Rejection, Leviathan and Jezebel.

The Arrested Spirit

Leviathan is the king of the children of pride. It retards spiritual growth and development, it impairs the senses, causes faulty judgment and discernment, so instruction and Scriptures are misunderstood.

This is apparent through the following: guilt and condemnation, spiritual schizophrenia, uncertainty about what the Lord wants us to do, and times with the Lord are wasted by distractions. Arrested Development spirits will blind and hinder people from understanding eternal salvation. To the Christian believer, there will be a genuine fear of losing their salvation.

The Arrested Soul

Learning disabilities, and the fear of the same, can cause inability to read, or hear what is actually said. The primary diagnosis is one of these: Dyslexia (abnormal difficulty in reading and spelling – including reversing the order of letters in a word), Dysgraphia (inability to write coherently) or Dyscaculia (problems with mathematics).

The Arrested Body

Physical growth and development are slowed down or stopped,

resulting in difficulty with normal body functions. This can include stunted motor skills, dwarfism, muscular dystrophy, Down's Syndrome, and more.

Immaturity in any of these three parts of our being will cause serious problems. Some live a life of disorder because they cannot make long-term and wise decisions. There is often a fear of being deceived, resulting in a hesitancy to try to walk with the Lord. Much of the New Testament is about growing up into spiritual and other maturity. John comments about the differences between children, young men, and mature fathers. Spiritually little children need reassurance about their walk with the Lord; young men need to mature as they overcome the wicked one and it's temptations, and it's the mature fathers who should be teaching them both.

About 80% of those with dyslexia are males. That seems designed to prevent them growing to maturity to give leadership in their home and family. The result are feelings of being inadequate, unprepared and unable to fulfil their responsibilities of leadership, so they withdraw from situations that would make them exhibit their maturity or lack of it. Jezebel is the main opponent in this area.

The legal grounds used by demons to operate in these areas seem mostly to include family involvement in Freemasonry, Roman Catholicism, Witchcraft and the Occult. Prayer and ministry guidelines for these are to be found in other books I've written that deal with these more specifically. *("Unmasking Freemasonry - Removing the Hoodwink," "Rome's Anathemas: Insights into the Papal Pantheon," "Unmasking Spiritualism: Supernatural Deceivers" & "The New Age: Old Lie in a New Package.")*

A very good friend reminded me about the Spirit of Confusion they discovered accidently for themselves. *"I have never been good at mathematics and don't understand how much of it works but one day after dealing with a spirit of confusion in myself, I could suddenly understand how percentages work and still do. I have done a lot of (ministry) sessions with people who suddenly feel confused. I bind the spirit of confusion and suddenly they can think again. It works every time."* They went on to add, *"Many times the issue may be rooted in generational stuff but it will be massively compounded by shame, stigma, hopelessness, confusion and rejection and fears."*

To show the effect regarding this, allow me to give a testimony from some very good friends of mine. The husband was a medical doctor, his wife a prayer counselor. They were asked to do some ministry regarding Freemasonry with a younger couple they knew from their church. Using a prayer guideline very similar to that developed by Jubilee, ministry was completed. Two weeks later, their eight-year-old daughter's teacher knocked on their door at home. That had never occurred before. The teacher said she was concerned with the daughter, as she had been diagnosed some time prior with a significant learning disability. But now, the teacher stated, their daughter was now learning at the same rate as the other children in the class, and she wanted to understand why this was. The only change in the lives of that family during that time was the ministry to deal with Masonic curses.

On another occasion, my wife and I were asked to prayer with the elder of a large Pentecostal church in our city. He knew there was Freemasonry in his family, and had some symptoms he thought needed dealing with, including Chronic Fatigue. Within the hour, that man had an amazing breakthrough healing. He then asked if we knew anyone in Britain who could do similar ministry. I gave him contact details of some folks we knew there. That group did intensive weekend ministry with Chronic Fatigue issues. Three generations of that family, the man's mother, his married sister and her daughter, all suffered from Chronic Fatigue. The mother and sister went to the weekend within a month, and all three family members were then healed too, including the young daughter who had stayed at home. Praise the LORD for liberty!

Chapter 8
Honoring your Parents

The term "honoring" means numerous, rich, honorable, to prevail and to be promoted.

Contrary to this is the term "Dishonoring," meaning weighty; burdensome, severe, dull and grievously afflicted.

"Honor your father and your mother, as The LORD your God has commanded you, so that your days may be made longer, and that it may go well with you in the land which The LORD your God gives you." Deuteronomy 5:16

"Children, obey your parents in the Lord, for this is right. Honor your father and mother (which is the first commandment with a promise), so that it may be well with you, and that you may live long on the earth. And fathers, do not provoke your children to wrath, but bring them up in the nurture and admonition of the Lord." Ephesians 6:1-4

"That it may go well with you" includes long life. I have never found anyone who seriously wants to be cursed. Everyone wants to be blessed, even when they don't fully understand that. I appreciate that some people have had such a bad life that lengthening it wouldn't seem like a benefit, but God sees long-life as a blessing. In fact, bad lives are frequently the outworking of curses - whether inherited or with wrong choices made by the person themselves.

Honoring, like love and forgiveness, is a decision.

The fundamental issue here is consequences. Respect and honoring begins in the home with parents. Then it includes school teachers, the police and other governmental authorities, all the way to respect and honoring to God. These are spiritual dominos. It is a well-known issue that people who had a bad experience with their fathers frequently have great difficulty comprehending the loving nature of a "Father God," because of the distortions on their upbringing.

Respecting and honoring parents provides us with spiritual as well as legal covering, especially when we are younger.

Let's not forget the lesson of Ham. He was cursed for mocking his father when Noah got drunk. While Noah shouldn't have allowed himself to get into such a state, Noah's other sons respected their father by going in backwards and covering his nakedness with a blanket. This is covered only page 33. See Genesis 9:20-27.

Chapter 9
Tithes & Offerings

Tithing is the giving of one tenth of gross income to God. Under Old Testament Law, God's people were required to give a tithe (10%) of their gross income to God, which went to provide for the Levites (their spiritual leaders). [see Genesis 14:20; Leviticus 27:30; Deuteronomy 14:22; Nehemiah 10:37-39; Malachi 3:8-10]. This included crops and livestock.

Now we are under New Testament grace brought by Jesus. We are no longer under the Law to tithe, but it remains a fundamental Biblical principle, and in fact the New Testament principles go far beyond tithing just 10%, and He commands us to give generously (i.e. much more than just tithing).

Both stewardship and giving are acts of worship. God is the owner of all things. When we give a gift to a ministry, it is one way to thank Him for His love and generosity shown to us. Our lives should be lived as acts of worship to God, including our stewardship and giving. In Genesis 28:16-22, Jacob realized that everything belongs to God, and he used his tithe as a means of worship

God's Response
God's blessing for obedience is in 2 Kings 4:1-7;
God can multiply the little we have, such as feeding the 5000, Matthew 14:14-21;
We will always have enough to be generous, 2 Corinthians 9:6-12;
Give and you will receive, overflowing amounts, Luke 6:38.

This is based on generosity not legalism! Do we look after our personal needs first, and then give God a slice of the leftovers? NO! The first share of what we receive belongs to God, and then we live off the rest.

All of what we have belongs to God, Luke 19:11-27;
God is given the first fruits of all produce, Nehemiah 10:37-39;
Honor God with the first fruits of your wealth, Proverbs 3:9,10;

If the rich cannot part with their wealth, they are not following Christ, Matthew 19:16-24.

One reason God asks us to be stewards and give is to test our willingness to trust Him. Our God who created the universe doesn't need the 10%, 20% or 100% of His resources that we return to Him. He can get the job done with us or without us, through us or in spite of us. His desire is for us to demonstrate that we are trusting, obedient and faithful in our relationship with Him.

The widow of Zarepath provided food for Elijah out of her depleted reserves, 1 Kings 17:7-16;
The measure you give will be the measure you receive, Luke 6:38;
Put your hope in God, not in your possessions and money, 1 Timothy 6:17-19;
Wealth is meaningless and unsatisfying, Ecclesiates 5:10;
Seek first the Kingdom of God and everything else we need will be provided, Matthew 6:19-34

The typical attitude is that we are self-sufficient and responsible for all we possess. The Biblical perspective is different – we are merely overseers of God's earthly domain, responsible for taking care of His resources until King Jesus returns.

We are called to be the wise managers of God's wealth, rather than the creators and consumers of our own wealth. In Genesis 14:17-24, Abram acknowledged that his victory spoils were a gift from God. We must surely know that God provides for all our material needs. He says in His word that He requires us to give Him a tithe so we may have blessings in our lives. Some people reject tithing because they claim it was under the Law, from which Jesus sets us free.

> **"Do not think that I have come to destroy the Law or the Prophets. I have not come to destroy but to fulfil. For truly I say to you, Till the heaven and the earth pass away, not one jot or one tittle shall in any way pass from the Law until all is fulfilled." Matthew 5:17-18**

It is clear that we aren't under the curse of the law, but Jesus is very clear that we still have the law. The matter now is this: Tithing isn't under the law. Abraham brought tithes before God gave Moses the Law. (See Genesis 14:20).

"For, brothers, you were called to liberty. Only do not use the liberty for an opening to the flesh, but by love serve one another. For all the Law is fulfilled in one word, even in this, "You shall love your neighbor as yourself." But if you bite and devour one another, take heed that you are not consumed by one another. I say, then, Walk in the Spirit and you shall not fulfil the lusts of the flesh."
Galatians 5:13-16

Actually, tithing is a revelation.

There is some confusion in many people and churches about this issue. There are some pastors and televangelists who have an eye on their own bank account when they bring up the tithes and offerings issue. I've seen enough of them to know that not all are honorable - some of them have a focus on the money because of mammon. Dr. C. Peter Wagner said in a private conference I attended that Mammon was a demonic principality whose primary task was to prevent the growth of the Kingdom of God by diverting the money that should be used for the Kingdom. He also spoke of the Spirit of Poverty that retards the spread of the Gospel. He said that the Spirit of Poverty is partly a mind-set; He said Poverty isn't piety; Francis of Assisi married Lady Poverty; and John Wesley also worried about having material things. This mind-set has invaded the church for too long.

Mammon isn't a synonym for money - it is a spirit. This includes companion Spirits of Greed; Spirits of Covetousness; Spirits of Parsimony - (Stinginess); and Spirits of Self-Reliance

How do we break the power of these off our lives?
Operate in the opposite spirit - generosity,
Give and it will be given to you,
Listen to the Prophet,

Delight in the Law of the Lord.

Sometimes a church leadership embark on a building program that is too much for their congregation to cope with. This can result in beating up on the sheep to make them give money to something maybe God didn't ask for in the first place. The mortgage is too big, or the costs of running their ministry have got out of hand while some live princely lifestyles rather than servant lifestyles. They become out of touch with the lifestyle of Jesus.

Having said all that, when we tithe we are not giving to the pastor, or the church, but to God. Get this revelation into your spirit and it will revolutionize your spiritual and financial life. Someone invested in printing Bibles so you could read it; someone invested in training evangelists, Bible teachers and pastors so you could hear the Gospel; someone invested in the radio and television programs and other media materials so you could hear and respond to God's invitation for eternal life in Christ Jesus. Someone invested in the Harvest for the Kingdom of God so you could hear and respond. If you know about and have accepted that wonderful offer from God, it is because someone else obeyed God in giving their tithes and offerings.

God will also hold accountable every church or ministry leader who wastes God's money on glory trips, buildings that are a monument to their own ego, or anything that doesn't advance the Kingdom of God.

Let us have a look at what God says to us about this issue of tithings and offerings.

> **From the days of your fathers, you have turned aside from My statutes, and have not kept them. Return to Me, and I will return to you, says The LORD of Hosts. But you say. In what way shall we return? Will a man rob God? Yet you have robbed Me. But you say, In what have we robbed You? In the tithe and the offering! You are cursed with a curse; for you are robbing Me, the nation, all of it. Bring all the tithe into the storehouse, so that there may be food in My house. And test Me now with this, says The LORD of Hosts, to see if I will not open the windows of Heaven**

for you, and pour out a blessing for you, until there is not enough room. And I will rebuke your devourer, and he shall not decay the fruit of your ground against you; nor shall your vine miscarry against you in the field, says The LORD of Hosts. And all nations shall call you blessed; for you shall be a delightful land, says The LORD of Hosts.

Then you shall again see the difference between the righteous and the wicked, between him who serves God, and him who does not serve Him." Malachi 3:7-12;18

So, tithing brings blessings, and the offerings over and above this defeats the devourer. The devourer causes your washing machine to break down one week, and then the fridge the following week, and then your car the following week, and then your clothes that are less than three months old fall to bits, and so on it goes. God has given us clear instructions how to deal with and overcome these issues.

The solution is obvious - we need to partner with God to win this world for Christ. We should also repent for only observing what God is doing instead of participating with Him in His outreach of evangelism and discipleship.

Dr. Derek Prince taught us that we should tithe where we are fed spiritually. I once managed a regional office of a Christian radio network, and there was one elderly woman who sent in an unusual amount faithfully every month. On one occasion I phoned her to thank her, and asked about the gift. She said that she was too elderly to drive any more, so had to walk to the closest church, which she said was fairly dead spiritually. But she was fed and nurtured by the radio programs. Quoting Dr. Prince, she said she tithed to the radio ministry, and gave offerings to the church she attended, and God blessed her. That is a revelation we should all prayerfully consider.

Chapter 10
Legalism
& The Spirit of Religion

The spirit of religion causes people to seek recognition for what they do, and what they are. There is a false and inflated pride in their position or influence. The spirit of Religion will always seek to quench the work of the Holy Spirit. If the Holy Spirit is in control, then the spirit of Religion cannot be. Actually true followers of Jesus Christ do want the Holy Spirit in control, all the time, for it makes for an exciting and eventful life. This means breaking with some things from the past, such as church or family traditions. The founding families of some churches are particularly fond of seeking to prevent change because it looks like their family tradition is being ignored or devalued. But nothing is forever, except God, so change is a natural part of what we all face, whether we like it or not. In times of much change, like our lives these days, can be a bit overwhelming for some. They seek to prevent all change, even beneficial change. Alvin Tofler wrote a book about this during the 1970's called *"Future Shock,"* and the issues are more relevant than ever.

Actually, on the issue of founding families being "ignored" etc., perhaps there is a need to more publicly recognize the benefits of those who have gone before, while acknowledging the need for updating things from time to time. Some of those situations, when handled carefully, could reduce the opportunity for the spirit of Religion to upset things through people. Wisdom and patience are essential ingredients for careful growth and maturity. The age-old issue of new and old wineskins, as mentioned by Jesus in Matthew 9:16-17, should show that some church structures cannot change enough to fit the newer needs of the people, and so maybe a new wineskin needs to be designed and commenced so people can get on with building the Kingdom of God. *(Much of my understanding on this topic has been from Chris Hayward, President of Cleaning Streams Ministries.)*

Demons never want to encourage God's purposes - their boss has instructed them to prevent anything God wants accomplished. The good news is that God wins and has His way, but He does allow Satan and his demons to buffet the people of God so we are battle-hardened, overcomers and victorious. Chris Hayward says accurately that demons will always seek to undermine any Christian leader who attempts to bring the fresh wind of the presence of the Holy Spirit into the Body of Christ. *"Many a battle has been lost at this juncture,"* Chris Hayward stated.

The spirit of Religion will:
Seek to gather people around the key person it is using;
It will seek ways to gain attention;
It will look for ways to subvert divine order;
It will seek to demean and slander legitimate authority;
It will claim it would be a better leader than those presently in authority.
It will pretend humility, while operating with pride.

It will major on minor issues, and minor on major issues. Tradition and image are everything. They are often impatient with church members in need, thinking they should have been more careful with their finances. The spirit of Religion wants to remove the true prophets of God, because prophets point out the truth, regardless of consequences. True prophets want to build up the people of God and do not seek to focus on themselves. Power and influence of spirits of Religion are undermined by true prophets of God.

Examples from the Scriptures for this include:
The disciples of Jesus were caught plucking grain on the Sabbath,

> **"One Sabbath Jesus was going through the grainfields, and as his disciples walked along, they began to pick some heads of grain. The Pharisees said to him, "Look, why are they doing what is unlawful on the Sabbath?" Mark 2:23-24 (NIV)**

Jesus was healing on the Sabbath and got into trouble with the religious people:

> **"Indignant because Jesus had healed on the Sabbath,**

the synagogue ruler said to the people "There are six days for work. So come and be healed on those days, not on the Sabbath." The Lord answered him, "You hypocrites! Doesn't each of you on the Sabbath untie his ox or donkey from the stall and lead it out to give it water? Then why should this woman, a daughter of Abraham, whom Satan has kept bound for eighteen long years, be set free on the Sabbath day from what bound her?" Luke 13:14-16 (NIV)

In Matthew 23, Jesus mentions the spirit of Religion by the description of how this works. Please look at this subject more closely, because this is one of the most significant causes preventing the work of the Holy Spirit in much of the Western church these days.

When Ritual controls our Relationships, this is Religion. Ritual minus Relationship equals Religion. The spirit of Religion is an agent of the Devil assigned to prevent change and to maintain the status quo by using religious devices. There are many spirits of Religion as we see in the many types of non-Christian and Christian religions both personal and corporate in the world today.

It is a spirit that is assigned to distract people from the truth by making them think that we are okay. The spirit of Religion is the meanest, most foul, most ruthless spirit that you will ever confront. It comes as an imposter masquerading as the real thing, cutting off believers from relationship with God and blocking the work of the Holy Spirit.

The fruit of the spirit compared to the fruit of the Religious spirit. The word of God says we can recognize a tree by the fruit that it bears - Matthew 12:33-37.

Second Timothy lists nineteen manifestations of the Religious spirit in the lives of people in the church.

"But know this, that in the last days perilous times will come: For men will be lovers of themselves, lovers of money, boasters, proud, blasphemers, disobedient to parents, unthankful, unholy, unloving, unforgiving, slanderers,

without self–control, brutal, despisers of good, traitors, headstrong, haughty, lovers of pleasure rather than lovers of God, having a form of godliness but denying its power. And from such people turn away!" 2 Timothy 3:1-5

The Bible describes two kingdoms operating in the world. The kingdom of God seeks to accomplish the will of the Father on Earth - Matthew 6:10, that is to bring righteousness, peace and joy in the Holy Spirit, - Romans 14:17.

In opposition to God's kingdom, the Devil has established the kingdom of this world. The Devil's goal is to resist the progress of God's kingdom and hinder God's plan of redemption. These kingdoms are locked in a conflict that will not end until Jesus returns and finishes it all. The Devil's goal is to counterfeit God's kingdom by offering the world a dead imitation of the true kingdom to hinder the progress of God's work by vaccinating the world against God's love. The Devil's counterfeit kingdom is called Religion. God's goal is not to create people who are religious. His goal is to bring men, women and children into a relationship with Himself and combat the spirit of Religion through love.

Some Warning Sings Of A Religious Spirit

Most of us are subject to religious spirits to some degree. Paul exhorts us to **"test ourselves to see if we are in the faith,"** - 2 Corinthians 13:5.

Please go through the warning signs below and check the ways you behave because you might have a religious spirit in that area of your life. Remember Religious spirits are seven times stronger than other types of spirits as demonstrated in Daniel 3:19. Remember that Religious spirits hold people in spiritual slavery. The battle against this spiritual slavery can only be won by unconditional love, in living the Christian life focused on Jesus and the Word of God and being filled with the Holy Spirit. So use this checklist to set yourself or others free to worship, walk and work with the Holy Spirit.

1   The tendency to see your primary mission as tearing down what you believe is wrong. This person's ministry will produce more division than lasting works.

2   The inability to take a rebuke, especially from those you judge to be less spiritual than yourself. Think back on how you responded the last few times someone tried to correct you.

3   A philosophy that will not listen to other people - "only to God." Since God usually speaks through people, this is an obvious delusion and reveals serious spiritual pride.

4   The inclination to see more of what is wrong with other people and other churches than what is right with them. John saw Babylon from the valley, but when he was carried to a **"high mountain: he saw the New Jerusalem"** - Revelation 21:10. If we only see Babylon, our perspective is wrong. Those who are in a place of true vision will focus on what God is doing, not on any human achievement.

5   Overwhelming guilt that you can never measure up to the Lord's standards. This is a root of the religious spirit because it causes you to base your relationship with Him on your performance, rather than on the cross.

6   The belief that you have been appointed to fix everyone else! The self-appointed watchmen or sheriffs in God's kingdom are seldom involved in building anything; they keep the church in a state of annoyance and agitation and may cause serious divisions.

7   A leadership style that is bossy, overbearing and intolerant of the failure of others. As James said:
> **"But the wisdom from above is first pure, then peaceable, gentle, reasonable, full of mercy and good fruits, unwavering, without hypocrisy. And the seed whose fruit is righteousness is sown in peace by those who make peace." James 3:17-18**

8   *A sense that you are closer to God than other people or that your life or ministry is more pleasing to Him.* This is a symptom of the profound delusion that we draw closer to God by who we are rather than through Jesus.

9   *Pride in your spiritual maturity or discipline, especially as you compare yourself to others.* True spiritual maturity involves growing up into Christ. When we begin to compare ourselves with others, it is obvious that we have lost sight of the true goal - Jesus.

10   *The belief that you are on the cutting edge of what God is doing*. This includes thinking that you are involved in the most important thing that God is doing. Again this is spiritual pride, self-centredness, even if it were true. Those entrusted with the truly important missions have the grace to fulfil them because God:_ see James 4:6.

11   *A mechanical prayer life.* When you start feeling relieved that your prayer time is over, or when you have prayed though your prayer list, you should check your condition. You will never feel relief when your conversation is over with the Lord Jesus - the One you love.

12   *Doing things so people will notice.* This is a symptom of the idolatry of fearing people more than we fear God, and it results in a religion that serves people instead of God.

13   *Being overly repulsed by emotionalism.* When people who are subject to a religious spirit encounter the true life of God, it will usually appear excessive, emotional and demonstrative. Remember how David danced when he brought the ark of God into Jerusalem? And remember this repulsed his wife Michal and she was barren from that day on, see 2 Samuel 6:23. Such a critical spirit will lead to spiritual barrenness.

14   *Using emotionalism as a substitute for the work of the Holy Spirit.* Do you think that weeping and wailing must accompany repentance? Or that one must *"fall under the power"* to be truly touched by God? Even though both of these can be evidences of the true work of the Holy Spirit, you are beginning to move in another spirit if you require these manifestations.

During Jonathon Edward's meetings in the First Great Awakening some of the toughest, most rebellious men fell on the ground and stayed there for up to 24 hours. Such seemingly strange manifestations fuelled the Great Awakening, since these men were truly changed. Even so, Edwards stated men who faked these manifestations brought an end to the Great Awakening more than the enemies of the revival.

15   *Keeping score in you spiritual life.* Do you feel better about yourself because you go to more meetings, read your Bible more, or do more things for the Lord than other people do? These are all noble endeavors, but the true measure of spiritual maturity is getting closer to the Lord.

16   *Being encouraged when your ministry looks better than others' ministries*. This includes getting discouraged when it seems that other ministries are looking better or growing faster.

17   *Glorying more in what God has done in the past than what He is doing in the present.* God has not changed. He is the same yesterday, today and forever. The veil has been removed. We can be as close to God today as anyone in the past. A religious spirit always seeks to focus our attention on making comparisons rather than simply drawing closer to Jesus.

18   *The tendency to be suspicious of or oppose new movements or churches.* This is an obvious symptom of jealousy, a primary fruit of the religious spirit, or of pride that asserts that God would not do anything without going through us. Of course, the Lord rarely uses people with such a mentality.

19   *The tendency to reject spiritual manifestations that we do not understand*. This is a symptom of pride and arrogance that presumes our opinions are the same as God's. True humility keeps us teachable and open, patiently waiting for fruit before making judgments. That is why we are exhorted to **"prove all things, hold fast that which is good,"** not what is bad, - 1 Thessalonians 5:21.

20   ***An overreaction to carnality in the church.*** Far more carnality likely exists in the church and a lot less of the Holy Spirit than even the most critical person would think. We must learn to be delivered from our carnality and to grow in our submission to the Holy Spirit. But the critical person will want to annihilate those who may still be doing things in the flesh 60 percent of the time, instead of helping them along the way.

21   ***An overreaction to immaturity in the church.*** The Lord tolerates a certain amount of immaturity. A four year old is immature compared to a 14 year old, but that is okay. In fact, they may be very mature for a four year old. The idealistic religious spirit only sees the immaturity without considering the other important factors.

22   ***The inability to join anything that you do not deem as being perfect or near perfect.*** The Lord joined humans here on earth and even gave His life for the fallen human race. The apostles that He called and released to build His ecclesia would probably have made most people's list of *"The least likely to succeed."* Such will be our nature, too, if we abide in Him. We will not just see people as they are but also for whom they can become.

23   If while reading theses signs you were thinking about how they applied to someone else, you may have a serious problem with a religious spirit.

Scoring On The Test

Score yourself on this test. Just remember that Paul did not tell us to test our neighbor or our pastor, but to test ourselves. Every one of these issues has applied to each one of us and probably a number still do because we have not come fully into maturity in Jesus. Also remember that all these are the fruit of having eaten from the spiritual Tree of the Knowledge of Good and Evil, and it takes a process of having our minds renewed to get free of the religious spirit's influence.

The Test Of A True Messenger

In Ezekiel 37 the prophet was taken to a valley full of dry bones and asked if they could live? The Lord then commanded him to prophesy to these bones. As he prophesied they came together, came to life, and became a great army. This is a test every true ministry must pass. The true prophet can see a great army in even the driest of bones. They will prophesy life to those bones until they come to life, and then become an army. In Jude 12-16 we see the false prophets as **"grumblers and fault-finders."**

The world is becoming increasingly repulsed by religion. However, when Jesus is lifted up, everyone will be drawn to Him. Because the whole creation was created through Him and for Him, we all have a huge Jesus-size hole in our soul. Nothing else will ever satisfy us or bring us peace but a genuine relationship with Him.

The Spirit of Religion

The Spirit of Religion must be confronted - it can never be left to control or manipulate the people of God, including those in leadership. It is bold, intimidating and ruthless, and it requires a bold, wise and strong leader to confront and deal with it.

While it will be painful and unpleasant at the time, personal and corporate growth and maturity will result from dealing with the Spirit of Religion.

If you compromise and allow it to prosper, you will grieve the Holy Spirit of God, and become frustrated with your inability to move forward into the things of God. The longer you wait until you confront and deal with it, the more entrenched it will become and the harder to get rid of. When Elijah confronted the prophets of Baal it was needful for a power confrontation.

This may also be necessary when we confront the same spirit today.

Call trusted believers together, and ask for wisdom, strength and God's strategy in this battle. Some people will seek to compromise because they want a quiet life. That isn't an option. It you want a quiet life now, you will have a terribly noisy eternity, complete with the **"gnashing of teeth,"** but if you will be obedient to the Lord now, you will have a much quieter eternity.

My friend, Chris Hayward, states the order to protect and move forward as follows: *"Proclaim the Word of God, employ the power of the Cross, and begin to take authority over every demonic scheme that has been assigned to you. Give praise and thanksgiving to the One who is in you, and who is greater than anything that is coming against you. Pray - and then pray some more! Pray before you confront, pray while you confront, and pray after you confront."* ("Freedom from the Religious Spirit" General Editor: Dr. C. Peter Wagner - Chapter by Chris Hayward p117.)

Matthew 23 is one of the best explanations about the workings of this spirit of Religion. We learn that it is quick to use its victims to point out the failures and needs of others, while being totally blind to their own shortcomings. For example, it often induces people to criticise others in areas they themselves lack, (verse 3). They expect more from you than they do from themselves. They also fail to see your need for assistance with the burdens you are carrying, (Verse 4). Chris states that one of the first places the spirit of Religion shows up is among those who seek recognition. Often subtle, it can be found among those seeking position, titles or power/control, (verse 5).

But God's recognition is all we really need, in His time and ways.

> **"So says The LORD, Cursed is the man who trusts in man, and makes flesh his arm, and whose heart departs from The LORD. For he shall be like a juniper in the desert, and shall not see when good comes. But he shall live in the parched places in the wilderness, in a salt land that is not inhabited. Blessed is the man who trusts in The LORD, and The LORD is his trust. For he shall be like a tree planted by the waters; it sends out its roots by the river, and it shall not fear when the heat comes, but its foliage shall be green; and he is not worried in the year of drought, nor will it cease from yielding fruit." Jeremiah 17:5-8**

How should we deal with the spirit of Religion?

First, **pray.**

Prayer is rain that softens the driest and hardest of soil. If there is a failure to change hearts on this, leaders must remove those through whom a spirit of Religion is operating from every position of influence, until there is a heart change. It would be more dangerous not to, and the costs will become considerable. Relationships will decay and cause fractures in the church or organization.

When people want to do business with God over these issues, there are three main steps to follow:
    Repent; (tell God you are sorry)
    Renounce; (promise God, with an honest heart, that to the best of your ability you won't do that again); and
    Break; (cancel and evict the satanic/demonic stronghold off your life).

There is a sample prayer you might choose to use to deal with this Spirit of Religion on page 73.

Let us not trust in our own good works or in a church or its leaders to get us to heaven - we need to trust in Jesus Christ - Messiah Yeshua Ben Yahweh!

Chapter 11
Unequally Yoked

There are some relationships, including marriage and business, that God won't bless. This is because these are contrary to His revealed will in Scripture. I personally know of many people who have entered a marriage or a business with a non-Christian, and I cannot name a single one that has been smooth and beneficial in the long term. Sometimes in God's grace the partner comes to faith in God, but this is relatively rare, and shouldn't be relied upon by those considering such a relationship.

This isn't intended to condemn those who became Christians following making such a contract or covenant.

> **"Do not be unequally yoked together with unbelievers; for what fellowship does righteousness have with lawlessness? And what partnership does light have with darkness? And what agreement does Christ have with Belial? Or what part does a believer have with an unbeliever? And what agreement does a temple of God have with idols? For you are the temple of the living God, as God has said, "I will dwell in them and walk among them; and I will be their God, and they shall be My people." 2 Corinthians 6:14-16**

In case anyone raises Hosea's case, this was a lesson from God to the people of Israel to show both His love and also their unfaithfulness.

> **"When the LORD first spoke to Israel through Hosea, he said to Hosea, "Go and get married; your wife will be unfaithful, and your children will be just like her. In the same way my people have left me and become unfaithful." So Hosea married a woman named Gomer, the daughter of Diblaim. After the birth of their first child, a son," Hosea 1:2-3 (GN)**

What part of **"Do not be unequally yoked together with unbelievers"** don't we understand?

Chapter 12
Perversion of the Gospel

Teachers of God's word have a great responsibility to get it right. Paul pronounced a curse on those who don't:

"But even if we, or an angel from heaven, preach any other gospel to you than what we have preached to you, let him be accursed. As we have said before, so now I say again, if anyone preaches any other gospel to you than what you have received, let him be accursed." Galatians 1:8-9

Paul also described a time when people would be more willing to listen to false words - it almost is tailor-made for our generation:

"Preach the word! Be ready in season and out of season. Convince, rebuke, exhort, with all longsuffering and teaching. For the time will come when they will not endure sound doctrine, but according to their own desires, because they have itching ears, they will heap up for themselves teachers; and they will turn their ears away from the truth, and be turned aside to fables." 2 Timothy 4:2-4

Moses wrote:

"Cursed is the one who makes the blind to wander off the road.' And all the people shall say, 'Amen!'" Deuteronomy 27:18

This pronounces a curse on those who deliberately mislead people. I believe this has a fair and reasonable application for Cult leaders and other false teachers. Cults have two main groups of people involved - the deceived and the deceivers. This Scripture would apply to the latter.

"These six things the LORD hates, yes, seven are an abomination to Him: A proud look, a lying tongue, hands that shed innocent blood, a heart that devises wicked plans, feet that are swift in running to evil, a false witness who speaks lies, and one who sows discord among brethren." Proverbs 6:16-19

I have noticed that people in churches who cause divisions never seem to prosper for long - God always has a way of causing the downfall of those guilty of this sin. I have seen it happen several times, including with people previously associated with our ministry. It was sad and avoidable, but some folk just can't seem to help themselves. Their destructive behavior affects others too. This curse also seems to work with the Spirit of Religion - see Chapter 10.

"Beware of false prophets, who come to you in sheep's clothing, but inwardly they are ravenous wolves. "You will know them by their fruits. Do men gather grapes from thornbushes or figs from thistles? "Even so, every good tree bears good fruit, but a bad tree bears bad fruit. "A good tree cannot bear bad fruit, nor can a bad tree bear good fruit." Matthew 7:15-18

"But there were also false prophets among the people, even as there will be false teachers among you, who will secretly bring in destructive heresies, even denying the Lord who bought them, and bring on themselves swift destruction. And many will follow their destructive ways, because of whom the way of truth will be blasphemed." 2 Peter 2:1-2

Those who bring a false word also don't prosper for long. When I have been in meetings where prophecies are permitted or encouraged, I often cringe a little when I hear some folk start off with *"Thus sayeth the Lord..."* because I know that if they are wrong, they are not only misleading their hearers, but also taking the Lord's name in vain with the resulting curse. One warning sign is if they start speaking in King James English. That language is over 400 years ago. Why not use everyday language? Since the prophets are subject to the prophets, according to 1 Corinthians 14:32, it would be best of people who were bringing a prophetic word commenced with something like *"I believe the Lord is saying..."* and then conclude with *"And I submit this word to the prophets of God."* I suspect we would have fewer prophetic words but those which are from God will come to the fore and could then be responded to as appropriate.

Chapter 13
Gossip

There are some who say that gossip is a harmless issue, but God's word says otherwise. If this is one of your secret sins, you must now understand that the Devil can control you in those areas that are secret, unconfessed and hidden. We know that light always overwhelms darkness. One candle or torch will dispel the darkness in the natural realm. Let us check some Scriptures to understand these issues.

"Therefore I say to you, All kinds of sin and blasphemy shall be forgiven men, but the blasphemy against the Holy Spirit shall not be forgiven men. And whoever speaks a word against the Son of Man, it shall be forgiven him. But whoever speaks against the Holy Spirit, it shall not be forgiven him, either in this world or in the world to come. Either make the tree good and its fruit good, or else make the tree corrupt and its fruit corrupt; for the tree is known by its fruit. Offspring of vipers! How can you, being evil, speak good things? For out of the abundance of the heart the mouth speaks. A good man out of the good treasure of the heart brings out good things; and an evil man out of the evil treasure brings out evil things. But I say to you that every idle word, whatever men may speak, they shall give account of it in the Day of Judgment. For by your words you shall be justified, and by your words you shall be condemned."
Matthew 12:31-37

"And even as they did not think fit to have God in their knowledge, God gave them over to a reprobate mind, to do the things not right, being filled with all unrighteousness, fornication, wickedness, covetousness, maliciousness; being full of envy, murder, quarrels, deceit, evil habits, becoming whisperers, backbiters, haters of God, insolent, proud, braggarts, inventors of evil things, disobedient to parents, undiscerning, perfidious, without natural affection, unforgiving, unmerciful; who, knowing the righteous order of God, that those practising such

things are worthy of death, not only do them, but have pleasure in those practicing them." Romans 1:28-32

"To speak evil of no one, not being quarrelsome, but forbearing, showing all meekness to all men." Titus 3:2

"But no one can tame the tongue, it is an unruly evil, full of deadly poison. By this we bless God, even the Father. And by this we curse men, who have come into being according to the image of God. Out of the same mouth proceeds blessing and cursing. My brothers, these things ought not to be so. Does a fountain send forth at the same hole the sweet and the bitter?" James 3:8-11

Dr. Derek Prince wrote that gossipers are channels through whom demons can attack a church. If this is a problem common in your fellowship, then the leaders need to deal with it appropriately, with integrity and without malice.

Let's be straight - gossip is murder with the tongue. Ultimately it will result in idolatry of self. This happened with a person who tried to attack both me and our ministry. They got themselves so deceived that whenever they thought God had spoken to them, they wouldn't let anyone tell them whether that word was true or not - self deception had so overwhelmed the person it was like telling God He got it wrong. Many pastors are particularly aware of this with fringe people in their fellowship who are absolutely convinced that God has given them a message. Even if those with discernment tell them otherwise, they are still convinced they heard from God and you can't talk them out of it. This is the effect of the self-idolatry.

"These six things the LORD hates, Yes seven are an abomination to Him...
A false witness who speaks lies, and one who sows discord among brethren." Proverbs 6:16, 19

Gossip frequently has the effect of "sowing discord" - by the fruit we know, according to Jesus. Sometimes this gossip is shared as a "prayer need." I have heard examples including *"Please pray for the pastor - his marriage is rather rocky right now,"* when there was nothing wrong with the pastor's marriage. This can be part of the discord sown in a congregation by coven members to ruin the pastor's ministry and the local church. *(More on that in my book "The Bride made Herself Ready")*

Chapter 14
Before Ministry

Before you do any ministry with someone related to these issues raised above,

- **Check the person is saved,** - John 3:16; 2 Corinthians 5:17.

- **Check they have been baptized in water, with Repentance,** -John 3:23; Acts 2:38, 41; 8:12, 38; 18:8; 22:16; & many more - NOTE: An infant doesn't know it needs to repent, so child "baptism" or sprinkling doesn't count - instead that is a dedication with water.

- **Do they have the habit of daily prayer and Bible reading?** - Psalm 1:1-3; 1 Thessalonians 5:17.

- **Do they attend a Bible-believing fellowship** where mature Disciples of Christ can minister to each other, - Hebrews 10:25.

- **Do they have an attitude of Thanksgiving to God,** - Philippians 4:6; Psalm 100:4.

- **Do they have an attitude of forgiveness to others,** - Matthew 6:9-14.

Once you have gone through these issues mentioned above, I believe you will find it helpful to prayerfully read through the prayer guidelines on the following pages, and then pray out it loud. It would be helpful - but not essential - if a mature Christian were present, and could pray through this with you.

Appendix 1
Generational Iniquity Prayer

It is best to pray this out loud, with or without a mature Christian present.

"Heavenly Father, creator of heaven and earth, I come to you in the name of the Lord Jesus Christ of Nazareth, your Son.

I come as a sinner seeking forgiveness and cleansing from all sins committed against you, and others created in your image.

I honour my earthly father and mother, and all my ancestors of flesh and blood, adoptive or step parents, but I utterly turn away from and renounce all their ungodly practices, sins and iniquities.

I forgive all my ancestors for the effects of their sins on me and my children.

Thank you, Father, for sending your only Son, the Lord Jesus Christ of Nazareth, to die in my place; to pay the penalty for my sins through His shed blood, and to bear the punishment for the sins and iniquities of my ancestors in His bruised and bleeding body on the Cross of Calvary.

Thank you that He is my Holy Scapegoat.

I choose now, to confess and take accountability for the sins through my family bloodlines back to the fourth generation, and to the tenth generation for sexual sins, known and unknown.

I confess and renounce all idolatry, known and unknown, also all involvement with occult power and looking into the hidden things of darkness by my family and ancestors. *

In the name of Jesus Christ, I now break and renounce all blood oaths, blood covenants, blood dedications, blood ties and all blood bondages to Satan and any other false gods by my family and myself.

I also cancel all ungodly documents, agreements and assignments against me and my family, past, present and future, and I apply the blood of Jesus Christ to cancel them. I declare their penalty has been paid in full by Jesus at Calvary.

I confess all ungodly behaviour, spoken words, thoughts and negative emotions that have had an ill-effect on my family bloodlines, on my marriage and other relationships.

I repent of all word curses spoken over or to others. I release each person from any offence caused, and release my rights to revenge, for the Word of God says that revenge is the Lord's only.

I confess the operation of rejection in my family bloodlines in every form, especially that which is now affecting me, my marriage and my family.

I confess any addictions in my family bloodlines, known or unknown.

I renounce the effects of any untimely death and any effects of war in my family bloodlines. I give to the Lord Jesus Christ all unresolved grief from these deaths, and from death of expectations. I ask you, Lord Jesus, to release me from the consequences of all unresolved grief and disappointments attached to the death of expectations.

I renounce all areas of false guilt and false responsibility in my family bloodlines.

I confess and renounce all religious restrictions and perversion of the Gospel in my family bloodlines, either from a Christian denomination or church, from a different religion, faith or tradition, or from cultic involvement.

I renounce any hereditary illness, whether physical, emotional or mental, and any other weakness in my family bloodlines.

I confess and ask forgiveness for any failure by myself and my ancestors for stealing from God by not bringing to Him our tithes and offerings as His Word commands. This has permitted the Devourer to plunder my family's wealth. I confess this grievous sin and I repent and ask your forgiveness now.

I choose now to be generous, so I break the curse and spirit of poverty off my life now, in the name of Jesus Christ.

I rebuke every related spirit, including greed, covetousness, stinginess, and self-reliance; and I command all such spirits to leave me now harmlessly on my natural breathing, and to go to your appointed place of judgement and not to return to me or my family, in the name of Jesus Christ.

I confess, repent and renounce any and all adultery, fornication, incest, homosexuality or bestiality which has been practised by me or my family bloodlines.

In the name of Jesus Christ, I now cut off all the effects of these sins, known and unknown, including all ungodly soulties, and I break every curse involved, in Jesus' name.

I also bind every spirit which empowered these curses and ungodly soulties, and I command you all to leave me now, and go to your place of appointment to await your judgement in the name of the Lord Jesus Christ

Father God, I come before you in the name of Jesus Christ, confessing these sins and weaknesses which may affect me. I release my ancestors into the freedom of my forgiveness. No longer will I blame them for how I am.

I now lay the punishment and inherited weaknesses on the Lord Jesus Christ of Nazareth, my scapegoat; on His bruised and bleeding body on the cross. I receive your forgiveness and release from their effects. Thank you, my Lord Jesus Christ of Nazareth, that I can cast my burdens on YOU.

Please heal me, renew me and lead me in your ways, that my life may bring glory to your name. Amen.

Appendix 2
Some British Curses

In the British Isles, the English were the most numerous and wealthy. Over centuries they invaded or controlled the Scots, the Irish and the Welsh. They built a navy for defence, and ended up with colonies on every continent except Antarctica.

On the religious front, Martin Luther's Reformation divided Europe after splitting the Catholic Church. Those who rejected the authority of the Popes of Rome were often labelled "Protestants" after Luther's statement *"I protest..."* For many centuries, the Popes of Rome claimed authority over all of Europe and the globe and it's people. They claimed the right to crown kings. Usurpers were challenged and often overthrown. The Reformation changed that,

especially in northern Europe. Princes and kings were more likely to protect reformers if the royal heads were influenced against Rome's control. When Henry the 8th of England wanted a divorce, the Pope turned him down. So Henry withdrew England from the authority of the Catholic Church and proclaimed himself head of "The Church of England." Nowadays they are known as Anglicans or Episcopalians. The Catholics fought back in various ways. One example was the attempt to blow up the English parliament with the King in it, known now as Guy Fawkes' "gun-powder plot." He and others were caught and executed for treason. The Pope also tried to use the Spanish Armada to invade England, but the British navy and storms saw the Spanish fleet destroyed.

Religious persecution grew across the British Isles. The Irish and others rejected Henry and subsequent royal claims to be head of the church, as they saw that position belonging to the Pope. (Later on, the Presbyterians rejected the claim of the monarch to be head of any church because they believed from Scripture that position only belonged to Jesus Christ.)

The Curses of Gavin Dunbar, Archbishop of Glasgow 1525

During the 1980's, I recall the late Dr. Derek Prince mentioning about a four-hundred year old curse he had dealt with in families in both Scotland and Australia. My research since has shown that the Catholic Archbishop of Glasgow, Gavin Dunbar, was so vexed with thievery and thuggery on both sides of the Scottish/English boarder that he pronounced a huge 1069-word curse on all those involved. These were known at the time as the Border Reivers.

"It was during this period of weakness, almost of total moral collapse, that the Archbishop of Glasgow took it upon him to excommunicate the Border thieves. Had the same vigorous measure been adopted at an earlier period, the result might have been more favourable. As it was, the launching of this ecclesiastical thunderbolt really created more amusement than consternation. It was regarded simply as the growl of a toothless lion. In no circumstances were the Border reivers easily intimidated.

Their calling had made them more or less indifferent to the claims of Church and State. They had never had much affection for the king, and they had, perhaps, still less for the priest. Having shaken themselves free, to a large extent at least, from the control of the State, they were not prepared to put their neck under the yoke of an ecclesiastical authority which even the best men of the age had ceased to venerate.

But the Archbishop felt that he had a duty to discharge, and he applied himself to the task with commendable vigour." "The curse was ordered to be read from every pulpit in the diocese and be circulated throughout the length and breadth of the Borders." (Robert Borland, minister of Yarrow. Border Raids and Reivers. Dalbeattie: Thomas Fraser 1898)

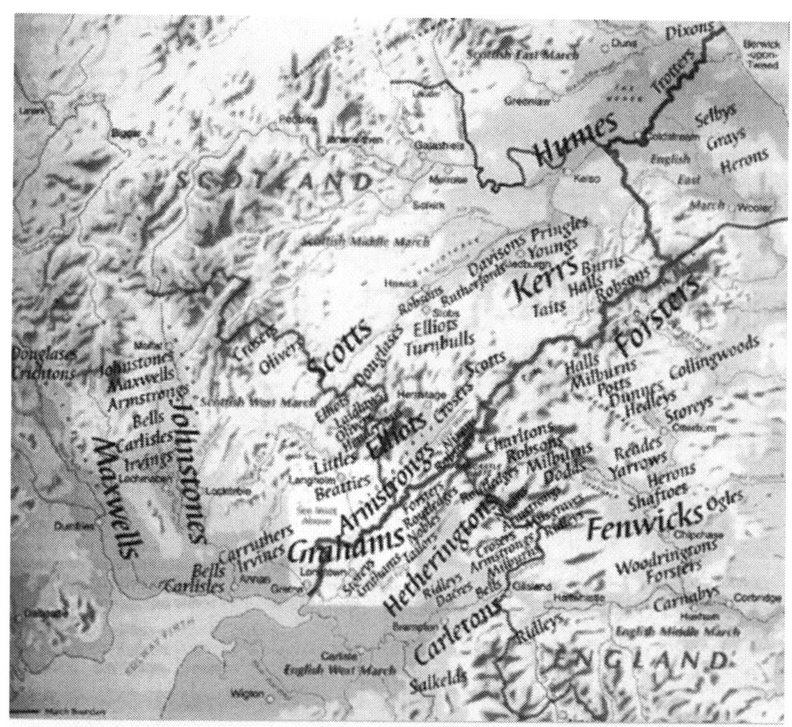

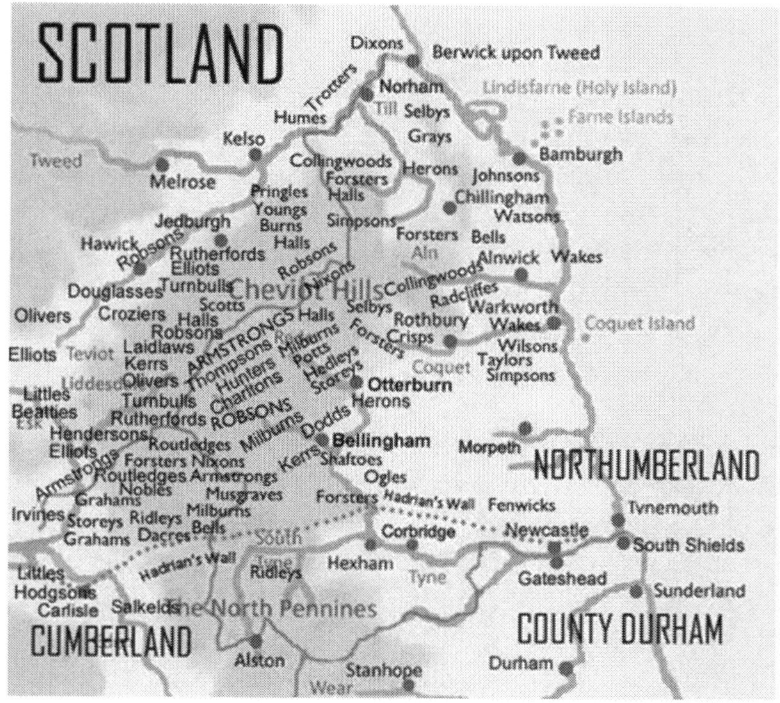
SCOTLAND
Dixons
Berwick upon Tweed
Trotters
Norham
Lindisfarne (Holy Island)
Humes
Till Selbys
Farne Islands
Kelso
Grays
Collingwoods
Herons
Bamburgh
Tweed
Forsters
Johnsons
Melrose
Pringles
Halls
Chillingham
Jedburgh
Youngs
Simpsons
Watsons
Hawick
Burns
Forsters
Bells
Robsons
Rutherfords
Halls
Aln
Elliots
Robsons
Alnwick
Wakes
Douglasses
Turnbulls
Cheviot Hills
Collingwoods
Olivers
Scotts
Dixons
Radcliffes
Croziers
Halls
Halls
Selbys
Warkworth
Elliots
Robsons
ARMSTRONGS
Forsters
Rothbury
Wakes
Coquet Island
Teviot
Laidlaws
Thompsons
Milburns
Crisps
Kerrs
Hunters
Potts
Wilsons
Liddesd
Olivers
Charltons
Hedleys
Coquet
Taylors
Littles
Turnbulls
Storeys
Otterburn
Simpsons
Beatties
Rutherfords
ROBSONS
Herons
Hendersons
Milburns
Dodds
Elliots
Routledges
Kerrs
Bellingham
Morpeth
Forsters Nixons
Shaftoes
NORTHUMBERLAND
Armstrong
Routledges Armstrongs
Ogles
Nobles
Musgraves
Forsters
Hadrian's Wall
Fenwicks
Tynemouth
Grahams
Milburns
Irvines
Storeys Ridleys
South
Corbridge
Newcastle
South Shields
Grahams Dacres Bells
Hadrian's Wall
Hexham
Tyne
Gateshead
Littles
Ridleys
Sunderland
Hodgsons
The North Pennines
Carlisle
Salkelds
COUNTY DURHAM
CUMBERLAND
Durham
Alston
Stanhope
Wear

The Reivers came from families who *"rode with the moonlight"* with their *"lang spears"* and their *"steill bonnets."* There are 77 predominant family names who can claim to have been Reivers.

Border Clans included the Armstrongs, Johnstones, Scotts, Elliotts, Fenwicks, Bells, Nixons, Maxwells, Kerrs, Dodds, Taits, Howards, Cecils, Douglases, Homes, Croziers, Forsters, Grahams, Irvines, Robsons and Storeys. These names are still common place across the Border country. The maps show the names of the families so involved. If your family is included, I strongly recommend you arrange to receive ministry for this.

The Welsh

The people of Wales were punished by England for the uprising of Owain Glynwr in 1402. These laws remained for 240 years. In consequence no Welshman could serve in any government or judicial position. They were forbidden to own any weapons or armor, or castles or fortified houses. Even food couldn't be sent to Wales from England without royal consent. England controlled Wales militarily, politically and economically, so the Welsh people and culture, including their language, were marginalized.

The Irish Curse

To bring the Irish into line and dilute their Catholic sympathies, the King ordered that thousands of English and Scots families were to be moved to Ireland in what are known as ***"The Plantations."*** This commenced in 1556 and continued for over one hundred years. Much land owned by Irish Catholics was confiscated and sold cheaply to Protestants. It's estimated that about 100,000 Protestants were murdered by the Catholics during this time.

The English Parliament enacted a series of Penal Laws against Ireland. Irish Catholics were excluded from most public offices such as law enforcement, members of parliament, judges, etc. Inter-marriage was forbidden between Protestants and Catholics; Catholics couldn't own firearms or serve in the military; they were excluded from voting; they couldn't inherit family land unless they converted to Anglicanism; they couldn't own a horse with a value of more then five pounds (to avoid it's possible military use); Catholic education was forbidden; they couldn't buy or trade to support their families; they had to pay a penalty for every Sunday they didn't attend an Anglican church; the Catholic Church was outlawed, as was the Gaelic language; and Protestants were forbidden to hire Catholics. Catholics who converted to Anglicanism could keep their land, or inherit the same.

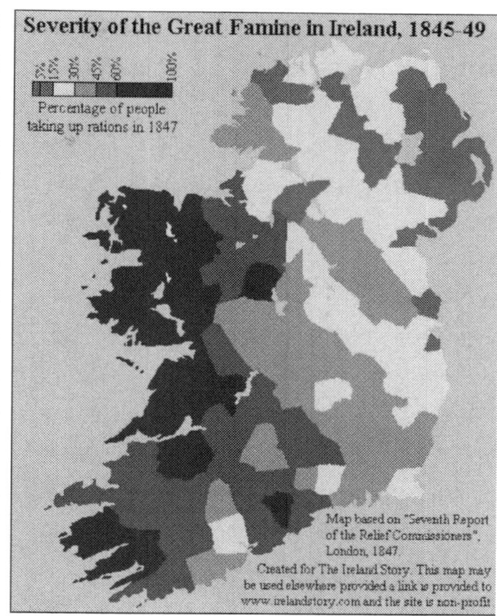

Later on, Presbyterians in Scotland were dealt with in the same way, including that Presbyterian marriages weren't recognised by the state.

One hundred years after Henry 8th, came Oliver Cromwell, who added to the persecution of Irish and other Catholics, and deported over 50,000 to the Caribbean as prisoners of war and indentured servants. The Irish responded with *"The Curse of Cromwell on you!"* to all Englishmen. During Cromwell's time, Ireland's population dropped from 1.46 million to only 616,000. So 850,000 died by sword, plague, famine, hardship or banishment between 1641 and 1652.

The English also rounded up petty convicts, political and religious opponents, prostitutes, beggars and unattended children and sent these to British colonies in the Caribbean and America, and when the later fought and gained their independence, to Canada and Australia.

The Irish potato famine struck in 1845 and lasted four years. Dependency on potatoes was more common on the west of Ireland, and at least one-quarter of that population died of malnutrition-related diseases such as dysentery and scurvy, and also cholera. During the 1800's, about a half million Irish moved the Canada, and almost three million to the USA. Significant numbers also went to Australia, and some to New Zealand.

What I've written above should give some clues why many of Irish extraction suffer to this day from lack of employment, owning their own homes, and poverty.

The Scots

Scotland has the dubious honor of being the origin of Masonry. The oldest known lodge is dated 1480, although there is evidence back to 1150AD. Information about this occult organization may be found in my best-selling book, *"Unmasking Freemasonry - Removing the Hoodwink."* I recommend the reader check the summary of issues on pages 107-108.

The Reformation was brought to Scotland by John Knox (1514-1572). His preaching and actions resulted in Scotland being declared a Reformed Protestant nation at the Treaty of Edinburgh in 1560. They called themselves Presbyterian - that being a form of church government.

James 6th of Scotland, who inherited the English crown and became King James 1st of England, merged the Scottish and English crowns. This is the James who instructed that a new Bible translation should be written, and it bares his name to this day. As a Freemason, his Fifteen Edicts for the translators colored the language used. Later on, his son, Charles, tried to impose the Anglican Book of Prayer and liturgy on the Scots, but this was strenuously opposed. By then, Scottish Catholics were a minority, but also suffered, as did the English and Irish Catholics.

The Anglicans of England (both royal and aristocracy) tried to force Scotland into their religious preferences. The Scots rejected the concept that the King of England was head of the church, claiming that belonged only to Jesus Christ. This resulted in the National Covenant of Scotland in 1638, proclaiming loyalty to Jesus' Kingship and His Word (Scripture). The Solemn League and Covenant that declared the preservation of the Reformation in England, Scotland

and Ireland followed this in 1643. Many people signed this in their own blood and added "until death" to signify how serious they were. (This action created a blood covenant and despite their best intentions, is a practise forbidden by God in Scripture.) This needs repentance to God and self-forgiveness to break this if it's in your family line.

The English king and the Anglican Church regarded these Covenants as treasonous. It resulted in violent persecution of the Scots. Wearing tartan, speaking Gaelic and carrying weapons were seriously punished.

"Understand that the Covenanters were not against the king. In their Covenants, they vowed to honour the king but only if the king stayed within the boundaries set for him by God. When he tried to go beyond these, the Covenanters resisted. The issues were the same as it was in Rome during the early church. Jesus Christ is Lord, not the King (or Caesar). Their duty was first of all to God and then to the king."
(www.providentialhistory.org/?p=600)

The persecution of the Covenanters increased, with many thousands of Scots tortured and killed mercilessly for their faith. These actions could be explained as Anglican aristocracy and priests persecuting Presbyterians and other independent Christians. Finally the English king (James 2nd) was overthrown and replaced by William and Mary from Holland, who were Protestants. They brought a measure of religious liberty to Britain.

Scotland was a patchwork of clans of related families. The landowners were like feudal lords, enabling rent to be paid and a militia to be assembled in times of inter-clan warfare, or threat from external forces such as the English. In 1746 there was the Jacobite (Catholic) uprising, which were defeated at the Battle of Culloden. (This was really a British civil war, not Scots versus English as often portrayed.)

Another spiritually significant issue arose for the Scots. These were entitled ***"The Clearances."*** They ran from 1763 until 1881. Huge numbers of these dispossessed people migrated to Canada, the USA, Australia and New Zealand. The English were only partially responsible for these. As late as the 1990's, over half of New Zealanders claimed a Scottish ancestry.

The Scottish clan chiefs, and the other nobles who were English, became convinced there was more income to be made from their lands by removing the peasant farmers (called Crofters) and replacing them with sheep and minimal staff shepherds. Many of the displaced families had lived in the same places for over 500 years. There is plenty of evidence of these clan chiefs and nobles selling their clan members (who they were related to) into slavery. The worst of them were MacDonald of Sleat, MacLeod of Dunvegan and Cameron of Lochiel. Many slaves were sent to the Carolinas in the USA. William Chisholm of Strathylass evicted almost 50% of his own clan. Colonel John Gordon refused aid to starving tenants, and those who wouldn't emigrate were shipped to Canada in appalling conditions, of which many didn't survive the journey. The Duke and Duchess of Sutherland were infamous for similar treatment of their own clansmen, aided by loyal clergy. *"The Highland Clearances were nothing short of the displacement and attempted genocide of the Gaelic speaking people,"* stated James of Glencarr. (www.clanjames.com/clearances)

Summary of British issues

During the 1700's and the 1800's, one way for a young man in Britain to earn a living (and maybe make a name for himself) was to join the military. It's well known that every British Army regiment had it's own Masonic lodge within it. That's partly why Masonic lodges spread so widely to British colonies around the globe. Corrupt financial and "land acquisition" practices by The City of London (the financial centre run by Freemasons for centuries) were often facilitated by these Masonic connections.

During this period, Britain suffered with as much poverty as France. But France had a violent revolution, and Britain didn't. The probable reason for this can be explained by the actions and prayers of Christian leaders such as George Whitfield, Charles and John Wesley and others, who sought a spiritual revolution with the Gospel of Jesus Christ, rather than a political revolution that resulted in the dismemberment of social order by violent means. It was also Christians such as William

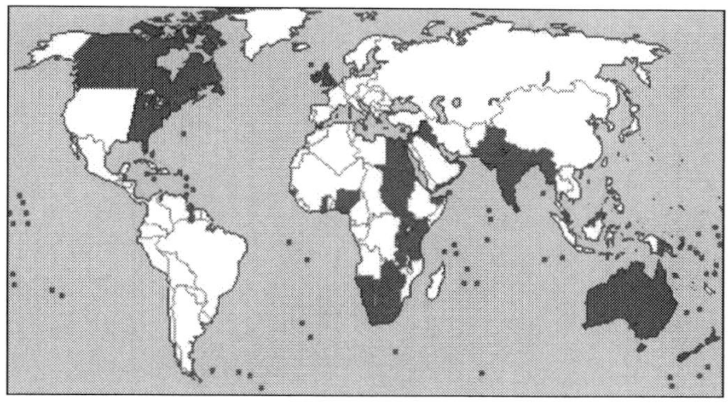

Wilberforce who ensured that slavery was abolished, ultimately globally, although many Moslems still practise it.

I note that India had a population of some 200 million at that time, yet the British kept law and order there for 200 years with only 40,000 military. British colonialism was not always wisely administered, but they do seem to have maintained law and order, built transport and other infrastructure and had a common language for commerce. While less than perfect, at least the British didn't leave behind the mess that the French, Spanish, Portuguese, Belgium and other European powers did when former colonies gained their independence by negotiation or war following World War Two. Essentially Britain tried to make those in their former colonies into little Englishmen, succeeding with some. Unfortunately many cultural expressions were often suppressed as a result.

In writing the above, I'm not trying to spell out every possible curse an individual or family may be enduring. Rather by providing some broad historical information, people can research relevant issues for themselves so they can resolve them. The above shows that Roman Catholics persecuted and cursed every one else, while the Anglicans persecuted and cursed the Catholics and the Presbyterians, and others. To the best of my knowledge, the leaders of those movements have never repented of their actions.

It seems there isn't a culture or nation without an antagonist to persecute or curse. If your life isn't perfect, I hope I've provided enough information for you to research and discern what curses you may be living under, and how to deal with them effectively.

Appendix 3 -
The Scandinavian Curse of Jante

In the 1980's, Norway was in a recession when Prime Minister Gro Harlem Brundtland, going on national television, declared an end to the Jante laws in the country. The prime minister believed that the ten laws of the Jante were destroying the initiative and self-esteem of the country. She read the ten laws and then proceeded to tear them up. Some people believed that this was an act of national deliverance and helped to usher in a spiritual revival for the country.

The Jante Law comes from the 1933 book "The Escape from Jante," written by Aksel Sandermose, which is a novel about an imaginary town called Jante. Sandermose, a Dane who lived in Norway, observed these ten laws in the social cultural mind-set of Scandinavians.

Ten Laws of Jante
1. Do not think you are anything special.
2. Do not think you are as important as we are.
3. Do not think you are wiser than we are.
4. Do not fool yourself into thinking you are better than we are.
5. Do not think you know more than we do.
6. Do not think you are more than we are.
7. Do not think that you are good at anything.
8. Do not laugh at us.
9. Do not think that anyone cares about you.
10. Do not think you can teach us anything.

The Laws of Jante describe a curse upon the Scandinavian people and I believe this same mindset is found in many Asian cultures as well.

This stronghold is similar to the Japanese proverb that *"The nail that sticks out is pounded down," (Deru kui wa utareru)* or the Hawaiian attitude of being laid back. In New Zealand and Australia, it's the "Tall Poppy" syndrome – being "cut down to size." The laws of Jante are not a Biblical definition of humility, but a false humility that is based on pride and fear.

The Vikings at their best were brave pioneers. When people are transformed by Jesus Christ and delivered from bondage to the Law of Jante, they take on this true spirit.

The Law of Jante has the effect of creating:
* An appearance of humility that is, in fact, pride
* A passive rather than an active faith (Fatalism replaces faith.)
* A lethargy that is difficult to overcome
* A lie that engenders a false religious spirit
* A uniformity rather than a true unity (Unity requires diversity.)
* A stifling of courageous leadership
* A resistance toward doing good works
* A legalism that opposes grace
* A spirit of judgment and suspicion rather than of Christian fellowship
* A cap on emotions, making a person feel emotionally restrained
* A climate in which prophets are not welcome

Prayer to Break the Jante Stronghold
1. In the name of the Lord Jesus Christ/Yeshua Ben Yahweh, I break the mindset that I am not special. The truth is I am a person of great worth because I am created in His image. (1 Peter 2:9)

2. I break the mindset that I do not have the same standing as others. The truth is God says I am good as anyone else. (Ephesians 2:14-18)

3. I break the mindset that others are smarter than me. The truth is I have the Holy Spirit living in me and He gives me wisdom. (James 1:5)

4. I break the mindset that others are better than me. The truth is God has given me purpose and destiny to be a success. (Jeremiah 29:11)

5. I break the mindset that others know more than I do. The truth is God is living in me and therefore I am connected to source of all knowledge. (1 Corinthians 3:16; Romans 8:11)

6. I break the mindset that others are more important than I am. The truth is I am precious and honored in His sight. (Isaiah 43:4; John 3:16)

7. I break the mindset that I am not good at anything. The truth is that God has given me unique talents and gifts to benefit others. (1 Corinthians 12:7-11)

8. I break the mindset that no one can laugh at me. The truth is that I live in God's love and acceptance and not by what others think of me. (Luke 15:11-32)

9. I break the mindset that no cares about me. The truth is God loves me and His children love me as well. (1 Peter 5:7; Romans 12: 10)

10. I break the mindset that no one can teach me anything. The truth is I am a disciple who is constantly learning from God and others. (Matthew 28:19-20)

I break the Jante Laws in my life and in my generational line. I forgive family members who passed down to me this stronghold or who may have wounded me. Forgive me for looking down on others. I forgive myself for believing lies about myself. Remove the cap that is over my life. Fill me with your Spirit to walk each day. Amen.

Appendix 4
Prayer To Be Released From The Consequences Of The Penal Law And To Be Released From "The Curse Of Cromwell"

"In the Name of The Lord Jesus Christ, I repent on behalf of all my ancestors going back to the root, of all hatred between the English and the Irish and the Scottish, and for all hatred between the Catholics and the Protestants. In Jesus' Name, I repent on behalf of all my ancestors for war, killings, murders, rebellions, destruction of land and homes. In Jesus' Name, I repent on behalf of all my ancestors for the buying and selling of slaves, for murders, killings, tortures, hangings and inhumane treatment of slaves or of any other human being. Lord, on behalf of my ancestors, I repent for robbing children of their childhood, for child labour and for child molestation and rape.

Heavenly Father, I repent for generational abuse and rape of women, and using women for breeding purposes. Lord, I repent on behalf of all my ancestors for renouncing Catholicism for the purpose of keeping their land and it was not a decision of the heart. Lord, I repent on behalf of all my ancestors for renouncing Catholicism for the purpose of inheriting what was not rightfully theirs. Lord, I repent on behalf of my Irish ancestors for denying my identity, for denying You, Lord, for blaming You, Lord, for our circumstances. In Jesus' Name, I forgive the English Monarchy for cursing us with the Penal Laws. In Jesus' Name, I forgive King William 111 and Queen Mary 11 and the English Parliament for passing The Popery Act, to ensure that the Penal Laws were more strictly applied. In Jesus' Name I extend forgiveness to the Monarchy, the English Parliament and the English people for stealing our land and our homes, for suppression, oppression and not allowing us to prosper.

In Jesus' Name I forgive all those who would not give us a job or feed us or extend mercy or charity to us because we were Irish Catholics. Lord, on behalf of all my ancestors, I extend forgiveness for forced conversions to the Protestant faith. In Jesus' Name, on behalf of my Irish ancestors, I extend forgiveness to the English Monarchy, to Oliver

Cromwell, to the English Parliament for cursing us so that we became a reproach to our neighbours, a scorn and a derision to those around us. We became a byword among the nations, a shaking of the head among the peoples. Dishonour was before us, and shame covered us, because of the voice of him who reproaches and reviles, because of the enemy and the avenger. Psalm 44:13-16 Lord, in Your Name, I ask that You would release me and my family and my descendants to a thousand generations from these curses that have come down the generational lines. In the Name of Jesus, I ask You, Lord, to release me and my family and my descendants to a thousand generations from the stronghold of the Penal Laws. I make declaration that we are allowed to get jobs, people are allowed to hire us. I declare we are allowed to own land and to own our own home. I declare we do not belong to anyone; we belong to the Lord Jesus Christ.

Lord, please release us from the victim spirit, the poverty spirit, the spirit of helplessness and hopelessness. In Jesus' Name we take back our identity, our freedom and our rightful inheritance. Lord, please lift off us the shame, blame, humiliation, ungodly brandings, markings and stigmas that came down the generational line. In the Name of Jesus, we are no longer to be shunned, we are no longer outcasts, no longer a byword among the nations. In Jesus' Name, we are released from the shackles of slavery and released from all contracts of forced indentured servitude.

I repent on behalf of my Irish ancestors for cursing the English or any others with the words "The curse of Cromwell on you." Lord, release us, our children and all our descendants to a thousand generations from the curse of these words, in Jesus' Name. In Jesus' Name, I break off us all chains, shackles and ropes that have kept us bound. I remove off us all generational ungodly limitations placed on us, I also remove off us all ungodly limitations we placed upon ourselves. Lord, I ask that You would release the blessings You have in store for me and my family and my descendants to a thousand generations. In Jesus' Name I appropriate all the work and power of the Cross for our freedom. Amen."

Appendix 5
Prayer of Agreement to Bless the Jews

"Heavenly Father, I come to you now asking your forgiveness for anything I have said or done that cursed the Sons of Israel (name specific sins if known).

I understand your righteous decree, that You will bless those who bless them and curse those who curse them. I now ask you to break any curses on my family or me that are there because of these sins against the Jews. I plead the blood of Jesus and ask to be cleansed from all sin and unrighteousness.

Heavenly Father, I submit to Your plan for my life and ministry that will bless the Jews. I also agree with Your plans and purposes for the nation of Israel. Lord, I want to receive Your heart for Your people, and the courage to do Your will, no matter what the opposition may be.

Heavenly Father, help me to humble myself and make the Jew first in my prayers and ministry to the lost. Lord, release to me provisions and favour to bless and protect the Jews.

Heavenly Father, confirm your message in me with signs and an inner witness of the Holy Spirit. In Yeshua's name, Amen."

Appendix 6
Prayer to Renounce the Spirit of Religion

"Father God, creator of heaven and earth, I come to you in the name of Jesus Christ your Son. I come as a sinner seeking forgiveness and cleansing from all sins committed against you, and others made in your image. I honour my earthly father and mother and all of my ancestors of flesh and blood, and of the spirit by adoption and godparents, but I utterly turn away from and renounce all their sins and iniquities. I forgive all my ancestors for the effects of their sins on me and my children. I confess and renounce all of my own sins, known or unknown. I renounce and rebuke Satan and every spiritual power of his affecting me and my family, in the name of Jesus Christ.

True Holy Creator God, in the name of the True Lord Jesus Christ, in accordance with Jude 8-10; Psalm 82:1 and 2 Chronicles 18, I request you to move aside all Celestial Beings, including Principalities, Powers and Rulers, and to forbid them to harass, intimidate or retaliate against me and all participants in this ministry today.

I also ask that you prevent these beings of whatever rank, to not be permitted to send any level of spiritual evil as retaliation against any of those here, or our families, our ministries, or possessions.

I renounce and annul every covenant made with Death by my ancestors or myself, including every agreement made with Sheol, and I renounce the refuge of lies and falsehoods which have been hidden behind.

In the name of Jesus Christ, I repent and renounce every opening, known or unknown, that I or my ancestors have given to every spirit of Religion in my family line.

I repent and renounce every spirit of Religion or religious spirit, and every work of darkness connected with it.

I repent for not fully receiving your love, compassion, mercy, grace and forgiveness; and I renounce any belief that You, Lord, are distant and judgemental. I choose to embrace all aspects of Your character and to intimately know you.

In the name of Jesus Christ, I repent for allowing myself to be led by any other spirit than Your Holy Spirit.

I repent for relying on my own intellect in worship, praise, prayer, reading the Bible - God's Word, and spiritual warfare.

In the name of Jesus Christ, I repent and renounce all legalism, traditions and religious formulas, and participation in dead works, dullness to the things of God, and hardness of heart.

I now choose to invite the Holy Spirit to lubricate my heart with His oil, and make it pliable to accommodate all the things God wants for me.

I repent and renounce every man's opinion of me where this is different from the opinion of my Heavenly Father.

I repent and renounce all compromises, of the truth, of my integrity and of my purity.

I repent and renounce all compromises in my attitude towards sin. I repent and renounce my lack of transparency for covering sin, not confessing sin, for not receiving correction, for being defensive and quick to justify and rationalize my sin.

I repent and renounce all deception and hypocrisy; all pride, arrogance and self-righteousness.

I repent and renounce all comparison, judgement, criticism, gossip, jealousy, covetousness, and anger.

I repent and renounce all persecution and slander of those moving in the Holy Spirit, especially those leaders God had placed in authority over me.

I repent and renounce every act of rebellion that has reinforced the spirit of religion in my life.

I choose now to have obedience to God and His Word as my attitude.

I choose to no longer partner with the same spirit which killed Jesus, and that continues to attempt to kill the work of the Holy Spirit today.

I come out of agreement with the enemies of the Most High God, and I choose to come into agreement with God my Father, with Jesus Christ and the Holy Spirit.

In the name of Jesus Christ I now break every hex, curse, vow, every spell, incantation or ritual, every covenant, blood covenant, every sacrifice and blood sacrifice.

I break every ungodly soul-tie, and every generational tie in my family bloodline which does not honour the Holy Spirit and His works.

In the name of Jesus Christ, I now break every other legal right, known or unknown, for the spirit of Religion to stay in my life, or in my family's lives.

I speak now with the Body of Christ to every spirit of Religion, and we say to you we come against you in the name of the Lord Jesus Christ, we rebuke you in His name, and we refuse to allow you to steal our intimate relationship with our Lord Jesus Christ.

I speak now with the Body of Christ to every spirit of Religion, and we say to you we come against you in the name of the Lord Jesus Christ, we rebuke you in His name, and we refuse to allow you to steal our intimate relationship with our Lord Jesus Christ.

We refuse to allow you to kill the flow of the Holy Spirit in us, and in our congregations.

We refuse to allow you to destroy the anointing of the Holy Spirit through us.

We choose to receive the anointing to break the power of the spirit of Religion in the Church of the Lord Jesus Christ.

Now, dear Father God, I ask humbly for the blood of Jesus Christ, your Son and my Savior, to cleanse me from all these sins I have confessed and renounced, to cleanse my spirit, my soul, my mind, my emotions and every part of my body which has been affected by these sins, in the name of Jesus Christ. I also ask to receive the perfect love of God which casts out all fear, in the name of the Lord Jesus Christ.

I ask you, Lord, to fill me with your Holy Spirit now according to the promises in your Word. I take to myself the whole armor of God in accordance with Ephesians Chapter Six, and rejoice in its protection as Jesus surrounds me and fills me with His Holy Spirit. I enthrone you, Lord Jesus, in my heart, for you are my Lord and my Savior, the source of eternal life. Thank you, Father God, for your mercy, your forgiveness and your love, in the name of Jesus Christ, Amen."

Appendix 7
Curses on the Land, & People, & Solutions

Christians want revival, but God wants Transformation. "Revival" speaks of a re-awakening of religious fervor. "Transformation" speaks of a change of form such as metamorphosis, or a sudden and dramatic change of scene on the stage. That means *"To make considerable change in form or appearance or character,"* (Oxford Dictionary).

Fundamentally I believe God is wanting to change the sinful character of a community, so His people can fulfil their callings and the Kingdom of God may grow. Sinful actions and words are empowered by demonic spiritual beings that bring curses on that land, and also on the people who dwell in that land. This applies to every community and nation, globally.

What is required for God to act? We need to know what we are dealing with. So far we have been looking at individual and church issues. Now we must look at changing whole communities. *(I wish to thank Dr. Alistair Petrie for his vital insights into these points. He taught this material to the Jubilee Resources' Summer Schools in New Zealand in 2008.)*

Four Major Categories of Sin on the Earth

These give legal right for demons to infest the area.

1. Idolatry Exodus 20:1-5; Jeremiah 3:6-10; 1 Corinthians 10:19-20; Deuteronomy 7:5;Jeremiah 16:18.

2. Shedding Innocent Blood, Exodus 20:13; Genesis 4:11; Genesis 9:6; Isaiah 59:1-3; Numbers 35:17, 33-34.

3. Broken Covenants/Witchcraft Numbers 35:33; Isaiah 24:5-6.

4. Sexual Sins, Leviticus 20:10; Leviticus 18:22 (Homosexuality; Leviticus 19:29; Jeremiah 3:1-2 (Prostitution); Ezekiel 16:25-27; Jeremiah 3:9.

Four Categories of Judgement and their Symptoms
Famine (Ezekiel 14:13)

      Not just food shortage, but famine for God's word (Amos 8:11)

      Loss of real identity

      A hungering for relationships with God and others

      Little harvest or blessing in the people's lives

Ecological Devastation (Ezekiel 14:15)

      Little sowing

      Death of productivity on land (Jeremiah 23:10)

      God controls rain (Amos 4:7; Jeremiah 3:23)

      God controls productivity of our labour (Haggai 1:9-11)

War (Ezekiel 14:17)

      Assault of a person, nation or group against another

      Divisiveness (opposite of John 17 & Psalm 133)

      Anger, jealousy, resentment, etc. between people

Disease (Ezekiel 14:19-20)

      Illness can be physical, emotional, mental or spiritual.

      Disease is usually caused by an open door of defilement, giving legal access to our enemy (Ephesians 4:27-28)

      Healing the Land heals the people on the land.

If and when people deal with these issues, as the Holy Spirit directs, change and improvement follow.

This results in The Seven Blessings for Obedience!
Ecological Health – Leviticus 26:4

      Higher water table levels

      Improved irrigation

      Increase in Natural Resources

      From Drought to "Showers of Blessings"

      Lack of unusual storms or natural disasters

Economic Health – Leviticus 26:5

      Food production, Trade and Commerce increase

      Higher export potential

      More purchasing power – no currency inflation

      Better returns on investments

      Wisdom and Prudence in business and Management

No longer held to ransom by other nations
Economic Strength

Personal Security – Leviticus. 26:6a

Lower Crime rates
Neighborhood fear evaporates
No more "No-go" or unsafe areas
Peace in the neighborhood
Fewer marriage or relationship disputes or break-ups

Civil Security – Leviticus. 26:6b

Corruption ceases
End of deceit and hidden agendas by politicians
Corporate and Work Life protected, Reduction of Red tape

International Security – Leviticus. 26:7-8a

God's presence and protection permeates the nation
Protections from greed of other nations
Threat of war or persecution removed
New Authority over challenges and impediments to God's vision

Honor & Growth – Leviticus. 26:9

Obvious sense of divine guidance and blessing
Divine favour apparent to other nations
Incomes exceed expenditure

Innovation & Creativity – Leviticus. 26:10

Untapped riches and resources uncovered
New developments in identity and commerce
Wealth sharing with individuals and nation
Prudence to produce much from little
Understanding of Godly stewardship
The Fruits of Healing – this results in Transformation.

Stewardship

A Steward is someone responsible for someone else's property, in this case, God's.

Stewardship can become defiled through:
1.   What we do;
2.   What others do to us;
3.   What our ancestors or predecessors bequeath us.

There are various stewardship issues raised by Jesus with several of His parables, such as the Workers at the Vineyard (Matthew 20:1-16)
The Tenants (Matthew 21:33-44)
The Talents (Matthew 25:14-30)
The Sower; The Mustard Seed; The Yeast; The Hidden Treasure; The Pearl; & The Net (see Matthew 13)

Stewards are Subjects of His Kingdom. God is the owner, but the people have temporary management and custody. The Hebrews didn't believe a person could own land. (Leviticus 25:23)

"To be faithful stewards of the land, we need to ensure that our position in Christ is not compromised by the manner of our work for Christ," said Dr. Alistair Petrie.

We are to be Holy – the People of God. (Deuteronomy. 7:6; 1 Peter 2:9 & others) Our identity must be in Christ. The old nature isn't to be resurrected.
The challenge for those who chose to be Holy is to get rid of those things, attitudes etc. which would defile that holiness. Check out these Scriptures: Joshua 24:14-15; Deuteronomy. 7:26; Nehemiah 13:8; 2 Kings 23:24.
Our commission to be to consecrated, and that involves removing everything which would cause us to be defeated. (Joshua 7:13) This requires obedience.

Examples of Stewardship & the effects on the land
Adam & Eve – cursed ground Genesis 3:17
Abel's blood – Genesis 4:10
Achan's sin – keeping idol Joshua 7:20-21, 25-26
Valley of Eschol – productivity of grapes and soil Numbers 13:23-24
Judas's Suicide – field of blood Acts 1:18

Prostitution – wickedness filling the land Leviticus 19:29
Fertile land becomes defiled – Jeremiah 2:7

The Three Questions for Inquiring Intercessors

1. Why does spiritual darkness seem to linger where it does?

2. How is the enemy at work in our church/community/city/nation?

3. What will we do about it (our method & strategy of action)

If we will seek answers to those questions, we would have a significant plan to change our community. My friend, Dr. Alistair Petrie, did a significant study on why revivals ended. Once a move of God has commenced, if we turn these issues on their head the move should continue as long as it pleases God. The character of God surely is for these to continue without end, so the main cause of these stopping has to be us, our failure to continue doing the right things.

Why Revivals End

1.   Lack of sustained prevailing prayer;
2.   Loss of persevering Leadership;
3.   Loss of personal intimacy or holiness with God;
4.   Compromise and Justification over sin issues within Christian   community and not dealing with footholds of sin;
5.   Improper or neglected stewardship (guard, keep and occupy or strongman returns with 7 more);
6.   Today's renewal can become tomorrow's tradition, lack of fresh vision of God;
7.   Cessation of Acts of Kindness, especially care for impoverished;
8.   Neglecting to Establish Watchmen – watching for footholds of sin;
9.   Not praying Godly gatekeepers into place;
10.   Allowing jealousy, personal ambition, denominationalism, misunderstanding or criticism to influence us and endanger unity.

This is intended partly as a warning so we don't keep repeating these mistakes.

Hezekiah did one of the best spiritual cleanup recorded in the Bible, in 2 Chronicles 29. Have a read and you'll be surprised at what occurred and God's response.

The focus of Spiritual Warfare is to bind evil and liberate captives. We have delegated authority from Jesus Christ, that only works when we are in relationship with Him. Otherwise it is mere powerless rituals or occult/demonic power being used. We must be clean enough to pick up the weapons and then to fall into ranks. We have a part to play in changing the results.

Where is a curse on the land, that places a curse on the people of that land.

One curse exported to much of the world, on virtually every continent, is Freemasonry. At it's height, the British Empire controlled a quarter of the earth (See map on page 89). Every British army regiment had a Masonic lodge within it. As Britain expanded over the world, Masonry was established, and in many cases still controls the governments that were set up over the past two-hundred years. The same could be said for the Spanish and Portuguese colonies that resulted in the nations of the Americas. Virtually every government in Latin America has had Masonic presidents, often continuously for almost 200 years.

Masonry has many spiritual children too, from the Shriners, the Orange and Women's lodges to Scouting, Cubs, Brownies & Girl Guides, (the founder of Scouting, Lord Baden-Powell was a Mason, as was Daniel Carter Beard, founder of American Scouting), plus the Ku Klux Klan, The Mormon Church, the Jehovah's Witnesses, and Christian Science, plus several other cults, were also established by Masons.

THE FRUITS OF FREEMASONRY - A SUMMARY

Fruit	Explanation	Scriptures show God forbids
Pride	Titles egotistical, pretending to be aristocracy or military of middle ages. inflated with self-importance BUT: we are called to be servants humble	Matt. 20:25-28, 1 Tim 3:6, Pro 16:18, Matt 11:29, Phil. 2:3, James 4:6 Isaiah 14:13-15.
Self-Righteousness	A member's proven character ages. standing in community required prior to joining. Brings vain sense of being good enough (by works) to stand before without a Savior.	John 5:38-40 2 Corinth. 3:5-6 Luke 18:9-14 Matt. 15:4-11 God
Idolatry	Local lodge leader called "Worshipful Master," "GAOTU" is not God of Bible, BUT: worship God alone, & call no man "master."	Matt 22:36-38 Exodus 20:2-4
Unequally Yoked	Members required to believe in a supreme being, not God of Bible. Brothers join at altar of pagans praying to false gods.	2 Cor 6:14-18, Ex. 34:11-16 1 Cor. 10:20-22, 2 John 9
Deliberate Deceit Dishonesty & Corruption	Leaders admit deliberate deceit over Blue Lodge members, despite ritual teaching morality. Ritual instructs preference to a fellow mason in business & society, regardless of merit	Titus 1:10-11 2 Cor. 4:2
False Concept of God	FM claims God is source of good & evil, also that Jesus & Lucifer are 2 sides of same deity. Represented in black & white flooring	2 Cor. 5:21, 1 Sam. 2:2 John 14:30, 1 John 1:5 Isaiah 6:3
Secrecy	Shown in much ritual, passwords, handshakes, etc. Many trivial, some embarrassing.	John 18:20, Mark 4:22

Fruit	Explanation	Scriptures show God forbids
Swearing Oaths	Oaths & obligations given 1 phrase at time, with a penalty invoking a curse, then ask God to witness what. He forbids.	Matt 5:33-37, James 5:12 Exodus 20:7, Lev. 5:4-5
Greed	Many/most Masons join hope for business, social or financial promotion, despite denial.	Titus 1:11, 1 Tim. 3:3-8 1 Peter 5:2
False Assurance of salvation	All Masons, regardless of beliefs, are offered immortality & heaven in Blue Lodge Ritual.	Rom. 10:9, John 3:16,18,19 Luke 7:47-48
False Resurrection	Ritual of 3^0 - Master Mason involves the ceremonial killing & resurrection of candidate.	Hebrews 9:27, Romans 10:9 Romans 3:10-12
Anger & Violence	The violence and ceremonial killing of the Master Mason brings fruit of anger, noticed in most Masons.	Proverbs 14:7, Eph. 4:26, 31
Spiritual Blindness & Searching	Every holy book is "on the Level" during ceremonies, resulting in belief that all religions are part of the true religion. Children & grandchildren of Masons often get into cults & strange religions/beliefs due to this inherited god influence, because any will do. The blindness is caused by the spirit invited in with the hoodwink.	Galatians 1:8-9,
Fear	Enters with the sudden noises while blindfolded; & with spear. compass etc. pressed into naked left breast during 1st degree initiation.	2 Timothy 1:7; Hebrews 13:6 1 Peter 2:17; 1 John 4:18
Curses	Arise from all the above. A curse without cause cannot alight, but these issues are the causes, so are justified by Scripture. Good News! The effects can be removed when the causes are renounced and repented of.	Galatians 1:8-9, Proverbs 26:2

A Personal Example about Curses on Land and Affecting the People

During the mid 1980's there was another of those serious droughts that afflicted North Otago. Growing up and attending schools in that region, I was very familiar with the lack of rainfall many years. Summers were very hot and dry, but they sometimes went on far too long. Average annual rainfall was about 22 inches (approx. 550 mm), but some years we received as low as 9 inches (250 mm).

One drought in particular had lasted for a long time. Local media reported that at least nine farmers had committed suicide. It was rumoured that their banks had told them to put their cheque books away as the banks wouldn't be honouring any more cheques. This was a very serious situation, affecting the whole community.

One Sunday, our pastor (Hector Bruce) said to the congregation that he sensed the drought had a spiritual root to it. He called on the church members to fast and pray for the solution. About six months prior, we had hosted a well-known Maori (First Nation) Christian evangelist, Norman Tawhaio. I recalled that Norman had taught many useful things but one thing stuck with me. Norman said that when the Maori (our indigenous people) named a geographical place in pre-European times, they did it with a Tapu. He said they would translate "tapu" as sacred, whereas, as Christians, we would see that as a curse.

Following lunch that Sunday, I got out my big Maori-English Dictionary, and a map. I started writing down the meanings of the various names I was looking at. Then I came to the name of the region, "Waitaki." The tourist books would usually translate this name as "weeping waters" in English, but there was more to it than that. I discovered there were actually nine different meanings to the name for that region. The last on the list was "proof against rain." It was like hitting pay dirt! I gathered up my papers and books, and headed around the corner to the pastor's home nearby. I showed him and his wife what I had discovered. Having pastored a large Maori church before coming to our town, the pastor and his wife both grasped the protocols and the revelation. We prayed about this, and the Lord gave a brief vision that in pre-European times, a Tohunga (a Maori shaman) had been walking along in the area and had been rained on. He got angry and cursed the weather. It did seem to make sense to us.

Let me provide a bit of background here. I recall getting a small book from the local library, entitled "The Maori School of Learning" by Dr. Elsdon Best, former head of the Department of Education for my nation. (The book was a reprint of an earlier edition, with the original being close to 100 years old. This book was published by that government department, along with many other titles by Dr. Best.)

In his book, Dr. Best described the pre-European practices of many Maori tribes. The main purpose of the book was to describe the training of Tohunga, or shaman. (The training of Tohunga was called "Wananga," a term often used to describe secular universities etc. This could explain why some unusual things are taught in some institutions.)

For Maori during pre-European times, this training required a test to prove competence. Having served as an apprentice under an older man, the test required three elements to pass. The first was to kill a bird in flight, with a word curse. The second test was to split a tree trunk or rock, again with "just" words. The third test was to kill someone using a curse. To increase their "Mana" or prestige, Dr. Best stated they often tried to kill their teacher. There were other examples used, such as when the sea tide was coming in yet insufficient food had been gathered; the Tohunga, with "mere" words, held the tide back until the tribe had gathered the required quantity of food.

Back to the drought situation. The pastor called for all the other Christian churches in the area to assemble to pray for the drought to be ended. So, around 7am the following Sunday morning, in bright sunshine with no clouds visible, we assembled on top of Cape Wanbrow (see photo next page) an extinct volcano that overlooks most of the main town of Oamaru, and much of the rural countryside. Despite some scepticism by some in the town, several pastors assembled, along with about 20 other people and a television crew. (Our story was one of the first stories shown during the main evening news that evening.)

One Presbyterian pastor present, known as being fairly liberal, suggested we should also pray for the drought that was killing many and inflicting much misery that year in Ethiopia. We all agreed and

then got down to business. We repented for the curse upon the land and the people, and broke the curse relating to the tohunga. We were gathered into a large circle. My pastor and I stood looking out over the town. At one point, I nudged him and pointed, without saying anything. He saw what I saw, and it was weird. On the left was a row of small hills, with rolling hills back towards the west into farming country. On the right was the Pacific Ocean. In between was a flat area with streets and houses. On the flat, but close to the bottom of the hills on the left, out of the ground poured a ground fog. It was about Forth Street. The fog came out of a circular patch and rolled down towards the sea, near the Woollen Mills, and then fell off the 20-foot cliff into the sea. It was actually like a river by volume. Within a few minutes, we were totally enveloped in cloud on top of Cape Wanbrow.

I had to preach that morning in a couple of different churches in the Lower Waitaki Presbyterian Parish. The minister was out of town and he often had me fill in for him. I knew quite a number of the people in those congregations. At the appropriate time, I explained to people what had happened earlier that morning. The pastors had agreed on the mountain that God had heard our prayer and would break the drought. I shared this too, and then gave a prophetic word (I didn't call it that at the time) that the rain would begin on Tuesday and that the drought would be ended by Friday of the same week. I also mentioned that we bracketed our prayers for Ethiopia at the same time. There were a couple of sceptical old farmers, but it did seem to bring hope to others.

It began to rain on the Tuesday following, gently at first, so the land could absorb it. Then it got heavier. The drought was declared broken on the Friday of that week in the local newspaper, The Oamaru Mail. And the same thing happened in Ethiopia the same week. You'll need to ask God why; there are some things only He can answer. We were just grateful for His mercy. The drought was over. That region has had dry spells since, but not like that period in the mid 1980's.

I discussed this situation with Dr. John Sandford (co-founder of Elijah House) around 2005, asking if the naming of a geographical place by native people with a "curse," was normal, he surprised me by saying he hadn't heard that before but it sounded accurate.

Since adding this material to my book, I had a conversation with a man who was a Police Sergeant in Kurow (approx. one hour drive up the Waitaki Valley) at that time. He told me the above event was in March 1986.

Why do I mention this situation in such detail? I believe it was because we fulfilled God's requirements! I recommend that folk ask the Lord for His leading when weather or other symptoms of a curse on the land in your region may need to be dealt with. What I've written above should get you started, and I'd love to have reports of results.

Appendix 8
Curses on Nations & Peoples

If you really want to know about the curses and iniquities in your nation or race, look carefully at what major problems are evident. Is there Anti-Semitism, or slavery, corruption, poverty, broken relationships, bad diets, state control/fascism, and more. Fascism is totalitarian, authoritarian, meaning everything is controlled by the state.

The following has been found in notes left by a very widely-travelled mature Christian couple who ministered in many nations. (They have both since passed on to Glory.) I have first-hand knowledge of many healings this couple were instrumental in. Without being legalistic, the following are issues they would look for as the Holy Spirit would lead them when ministering to folks from the following nations/people-groups.

English: Druids, Death, Hangman, Beheading, Witch, Freemasonry, Serfdom, Scullery Maid, Arthritis, Hemochromatosis (too much iron in blood from cooking pots), Castles, Invasion by the Spanish, Invasion by the Normans, Arrogance, Stoicism, Stubbornness, Maypole, Confusion.

Irish: above plus, Catholicism, Freemasonry, Uncontrollable anger, Religious, Rebellion, Bloodshed, Warring Spirits, Pride of "the Fighting Irish," Put-down, Alcoholism, Lewd Jokes, Poverty, Bog Irish, Destitution, Despair, Starvation, Potato Famine, Superstition.

Scots: As English above, plus, Stingy, False Frugality, Rejection, Poverty, Meanness, Unforgiveness (clan against clan), Pride, Freemasonry, Warring Spirits, (Murder/Blood Oaths) Family Divisions and hate, Celts, Homosexuality.

Welsh: as English and Irish, plus, Bronchial Problems (black lung from coal mines), Melancholy, Addictions, Antagonism, Sport Idolatry, Matriarchal Control, Druids.

Dutch: Incest (in a certain group), Destruction of Children, Euthanasia, Arrogance, False Pride, German Invasion, Perfectionism, Drugs, Stubbornness, Secretive, Difficult, Bluntness, Harshness, Permissiveness, Prostitution, Workaholism.

Belgian: Temper, Stubbornness, Independence, Child Abuse (Some Dutch may apply).

German: Rebellion (1 Samuel 15:23 = witchcraft), Stubbornness, Pride, Anti-Semitism, Murder, Cruelty, Superiority, Control, Legalism, Gloom, Lethargy, Serfdom, Burden-bearer, Asthma, Incest, Arrogance, Curses from Jews because of Holocaust, Anorexia, Poverty, Crippling (knee, back & ankle problems), "experimental kitchen" surgeries, Illness, Infirmity, Family Division.

Gypsies: Gross Rejection, Physical & Emotional Abuse, Wandering, Homelessness, Mistrust, Lying, Thievery, Poverty, False gods, Occult (bind "3rd eye"), Enslavement, Unemployment, Humiliation, Illiteracy, Criminal, Holocaust, Forced cannibalism, Gassing experiments, Sterilization, Genocide, Starvation, Premature Death.

Jewish: Hate, Anti-Christ (inability to Worship Jesus/Yeshua), Compulsive hand-washing, Victimization, Curse of the Law, Premature death, Curse on their Blood (Taysac's Disease), Breathing Difficulties/Suffocation, Dread/Fear, Inability to stay in bed.

Poland: Chronic Fatigue Syndrome, German Invasion.

Hungarian: Attila the Hun (1000AD) Oppression, Cruelty.

Slovenian: Cursing, Swearing, Alcoholism, Communism, Generational Child Abuse (physical).

Kosovo: Oppression (by Ottoman Turks & others), Darkness, Genocide, Cruelty, Death, Division, Death of males by Serbians plus rape.

Ukraine: Can't breathe, Asthma, Starvation, Division of Families, Oppression.

Macedonian: Religious Spirits, Icons, Idolatry, Oppression by Ottoman Turks & others.

Greek: As Above, Anti-Christ, False Gods, Mythology, Pride, Superiority, Arrogance, Control (by men & older women), Spartan's Brutality, Bloodshed, Discontent, Distress, Fear.

Italian: Lawlessness, Thieving, Murder, Control, Lust, Sicilian/Mafia, Poverty, Religious Spirits, Inquisition, Screaming, Anti-Semitism, Persecution of Christians, Screaming Fishwives.

Maltese: Anger, Control, Alcoholism.

Spain: Lust (for power, wealth, blood), Inquisition, Conquistadors – Fighting, Torture, Cruelty, Catholicism, Control, Cruelty, Armada, Invasion, Division, Deception, Trickery, Materialism, Immorality.

French: Haughtiness, Lust, Huguenots = warring, Persecution of Christians, Anti-Christ, Division, Stubbornness, Stoicism, Normandy Invaders.

Danish: Cruelty, Promiscuity, Jante, Rejection, Materialism, Freemasonry.

Swedish: Euthanasia, Suicide, Humanism, Socialism, Mythology, Freemasonry, Jante, Lust, Incest.

Norwegian: Vikings, Pride of Heritage, Cruelty, Rape, Knees (kneeling in snow begging for life), Anti-Christ, Mythology, Valhalla, Wolf, Spirit Guides, Trickery, Gnomes, Trolls, Freemasonry, Jante, Occultism.

Finland: Rejection, Self-Rejection, Matriarchal, Unforgiveness, Depression, Alcoholism, Jante, Superstition.

Switzerland: Independence, Materialism, Secretive (especially in Banking), Emotional Coldness, Racial Friction (between German, French & Italian communities), New Age, Witchcraft, Occultism, Greed.

Russian: Alcoholism, Poverty, Anti-Semitism, Fighting, Abortion, Death, Communism, Cruelty, Atheism, Idolatry, Anti-Christ, Witchcraft, New Age, Serfdom, Inferiority, Fascism.

Kazakhstan: Abortion, Murder, Death (proclaim Psalm 118:17).

Australian: Freemasonry, "Down Under," Penal Colony, Criminal, Unconcern for life, Abortion, Murder, Suicide, Incest, Tall Poppy Syndrome, Low Self-esteem, Lackadaisical - "She'll be right," Materialism, Freemasonry, Self-Indulgence, Poverty, Gambling, Stubbornness, Stoicism, Alcoholism, Rebellion, Rejection, Jealousy, Abandonment, (women jailed & their babies put out on streets).

Australian Aborigines: False gods, Sign of the Serpent, Gross rejection, Mistrust, Negativism, Sexual Abuse, Incest, Walkabout Spirit, Dream-time, Totem, Didgeridoo (instrument used by men to call up demons – women cursed if they blow it), Bad Temper, Unreality, Pointing Bones (to curse to death), Alcoholism, Unforgiveness, Unacceptance, Genocide, Fragmentation, Cruelty, Curses, Homeless/Wandering, Insecurity, Humiliation, Stolen Children, Rebellion, False Identity, Loss of Identity, Self-Abuse, Rape, Hate (90% of those in Tasmania were killed).

New Zealand: Freemasonry, Apathy, Lackadaisical - "She'll be right," False Pride, Lower Self-Esteem, Suicide, Child Abuse, New Age, Escapism.

New Zealand Maori: Rejection, Revenge (Utu), False gods, Cannibalism, Brutality, Warring Spirits, Necromancy, Mistrust, Incest, Physical Abuse, Cruelty, Alcoholism, Forced from land.

Papua New Guinea: Alcoholism, Gambling, Beetle Nuts, Nicotine, Necromancy, Fear, Superstition, Voodoo, Witchcraft, Occult, Idolatry, Japanese Occupation, Asthma, Transference, Bad Backs, Knee Problems, High Blood Pressure, Diabetes, Abandonment, Desertion, Poverty, Illegitimacy, Death, Rejection, Self-Destruction.

Fiji: Premature Death (lifespan 45-50), Fear, Asthma, Poverty, Strife, Hate between Fijians & Indians, Laziness, Futility.

Polynesian: Worship of False gods, Idolatry (with human sacrifices to "island spirits"), Occultism, Rejection, Anger, Corruption, Mormonism, Drunkenness, Superstition.

Tahitian: As Above, French Bloodlines possible).

Hawaiian: As above, plus Chinese & Japanese.

Chinese: Buddhism, Ancestor Worship, Anti-Christ, Martial Arts (power demons & spirit guides), Death, Guilt, Abortion, Murder, Rejection of Females, Abuse by Mothers-in-law, Communism, State Control.

Japan: Shintoism, Buddhism, Taoism, Pride (personal, family & national), Fear of Man, Fear of Public Disgrace, Gambling, Suicide, Workaholism, Abortion, Lust, Jealousy.

India: False gods, Anti-Christ, Idol Worship, Darkness, Poverty, British Occupation, Hinduism, Caste System causing hopelessness, Heart Problems, Occult (blind the "third eye" Horus), Serpent spirits (Shiva, Kali, Kundalini).

Malaysia: Rejection, Colonialism, Superiority, Islamic Domination, Fear of Authority, Fortune-telling, Occultism & Witchcraft, Animism, Apathy, Corruption, Materialism, Jealousy.

Philippines: Rejection, Foreign Domination, Bribery, Corruption, Alcoholism, Matriarchal Domination, Theft, Bestiality, Occultism, Catholicism, Icons, Saints, Black Pope, Islam, Poverty, Superstition.

Vietnam: Communism, Anti-Christ, Strong Rejection, Anger, Violence, Murder, Wandering (Vagabond curse), Death, Crippling, Destruction, Trauma, Fear, US & Allied Veterans – Buddhist curse.

Thailand: Rejection, Violence, Buddhism, Spirit Worship, Lust, Adultery, Prostitution (including children), Corruption, Alcoholism, Gambling, Apathy

Turkey/Persia/Iran: Islam, Death, Murder, Slavery, Cruelty, Generational Hatred, Covetousness, Jealousy, Ottoman Empire & Genocide.

America: National Pride & Arrogance, Self-reliance, Self-centred, Materialism, Abortion, Gluttony, Religious Legalism, Religious Deception/Cults, Freemasonry, Fantasy (Hollywood), Racism, Ku Klux Klan, Occultism.

American Indians: False gods, Treachery, TB, Occult, Spirit Guides, Suicide, Hopelessness, Tribal & self-mutilation, Mistrust, Sexual Abuse, Rape, Addiction, Alcoholism, Drugs, Cruelty, "Trail of Tears", Oppression, Self-sacrificing, Totems.

Mexico: Catholicism, Poverty, Idolatry, Grand Orient Freemasonry, Materialism, Pride & Arrogance, Occultism, Day of Death, Bestiality, Child & Animal Sacrifices.

Brazil: Cannibalism, Promiscuity, Occultism, Witchcraft, Voodoo, Murder, Fear, Idolatry, Racism.

Peru: Poverty, Inca gods, Sun gods, Paganism, Futility, Hopelessness, Fear, Spanish Invasion, Feet Knees & Backs, Human Sacrifices, Destruction of family, Unforgiveness, Fortune telling, Witchcraft, Bribery, Stealing, Drugs, Alcohol, Depression, Oppression, Misery, Rebellion, Disobedience, Mind Control, Necromancy, Lying, Adultery, Prostitution, Barrenness, Aids, Gangs, Fornication, Rape, Perversion, Lust, Suicide, Condemnation.

Honduran: Poverty, Hopelessness, Futility, Darkness, Witchcraft, Voodoo, Occult, Burden-bearer.

Haitian: As above, plus African & French. (This country dedicated to Satan over 200 years ago, this curse broken over Haiti August 1997.) Voodoo as a national religion. People still under this curse.

Jamaican: Darkness, Witchcraft, Voodoo, Poverty, Occult.

Puerto Rico: Darkness, Bondage, Poverty, Occult, Santeria.

Cuba: As above, plus Communism.

Arabs: Rejection, Aggressive, Antagonism, Wild, Loveless, Covert Homosexuality, Superstition, Occultism, Lying & Deceit, Male Supremacy/Misogyny,

Africa: Colonisation, Rejection, Idolatry, Superstition, Rebellion, Poverty,

Corruption, Freemasonry, Sex with Demons, Polygamy, Adultery, Bondage, Slavery, Witchcraft, Occult, Voodoo, Sickle-cell Anaemia, Aids, Hatred, Murder, Cannibalism, Theft, Drugs, Treachery, Racism Syndrome, Fear, Jungle Beat Dancing, Civil Wars, Witch-doctors.

South Africa: Apartheid, Dutch Rule, Boer War, Rejection, Self-Rejection, Violence, Rebellion, Racial Prejudice, Religious Legalism, Witchcraft, Poverty, Zulu Wars, Argumentative.

Egyptian: Anti-Christ, False gods, Cruelty, Plagues, Occult, Curses from enslaved Israelites, Cobra spirit (Anulifera), Killing of babies, Shaking Screams.

We'll know the Kingdom of God is really advancing when these types of ministry are being taught and used in every Bible College or Seminary and EVERY congregation of believers in Jesus Christ that claims the title "Christian."

About Jubilee Resources International

God's commission for Jubilee Resources International is based on Ezekiel 33:1-9, and Luke 4:18-21. According to the Bible, Jubilee years were times of restitution. Debts were cancelled, slaves set free, families reunited and lost or forfeited inheritances restored. Every year was prophetic of the ministry of Jesus Christ. The Jubilee was proclaimed on the basis of the work of the High Priest on the Day of Atonement - so Jesus Christ's liberating ministry is founded on His atoning work. Jesus began His public ministry by reading the passage from the prophet Isaiah (Luke 4:18-21). All the liberties of the Jubilee year are now available to us through the redemptive work of Jesus Christ at Calvary, and we all have the responsibility to preach this Gospel of Redemption and Restoration to full Relationship with Yahweh/Father God. When Yeshua/Jesus Christ returns, God's people will be totally free from all sin, sickness and disease, death and curse. The Biblical Jubilee will then be fully realized.

Resources in print book, eBook, audio & video formats are available in English, with paper & eBooks in Spanish, German, French, Italian, Portuguese-Brazil, Polish, Russian, Dutch, Swedish, Danish, Finnish, Hungarian, Romanian, Slovak, Czech, Greek, Afrikaans & Tagalog, with other languages pending.

About the Author:
Selwyn R. Stevens,
Ph.D; D.Min.; M.I.S.D.M.; M.E.A.C.M.

is the President of Jubilee Resources International Inc. a New Zealand-based educational and religious organization involved in informing and equipping Christians of all denominations how to reach the lost and deceived in cults, the occult and secret societies such as Freemasonry. Author of over 35 books (and co-author of two), including twelve Best Sellers, an International Speaker (on five continents) and ordained minister. Dr. Stevens is a third-generation preacher, and has been involved in various Christian groups, and also maintains an active interest in national and world affairs and politics. Dr. Stevens is a Foundation Member of the International Society of Deliverance Ministers, founded by Dr. C. Peter Wagner and convened by Dr. William Sudduth of Virginia, USA; and Apostolic Overseer of the Alliance of African Christian Churches & Ministries based in Zambia. Regular Facebook and e-mail teaching and mentoring is also provided to many Christian leaders across Africa, Asia, Caribbean & Latin America, resulting in tens of thousands being equipped for service to the Kingdom of God.

Additional Resources Available by
Selwyn R. Stevens

www.jubileeresources.org (Webshop)
Plus comprehensive range of free tracts to download

Dealing with Curses & Generational Iniquities. This teaching offers hope for all Christians that they can be released into the blessings of God and forever leave behind iniquities and curses that have kept them captive, perhaps their whole families for generations. This explains the twelve major curses that people may have operating in their families, and what to do about them. It also includes new material on the curses over Scottish, English, Irish, Welsh and Scandinavian people, plus many other national and ethnic groups. This teaching has been taught in several nations with much fruit for personal, family and community liberty. Best Seller
Book, E-book, MP4 & DVD

Dealing with Demons: *Insights into evil spiritual influences.* This popular teaching provides outstanding insights regarding evil spiritual influences that exist in the world in which we live today, and then goes further to show us what to do about it. Best Seller
Book, E-book, MP4 & DVD

Insights into Martial Arts, Tai Ch'i TM & Yoga. Much of the western world has seen an explosion of these practices. For many, their involvement has became close to a religion, adopting belief systems, mind sets and practises inconsistent with the teachings of the Bible. Best Seller
Book, E-book, MP4 & DVD

Treated or Tricked - Alternative Health Therapies Diagnosed. Many people are now trying Alternative Health Therapies. This book explains the various medical & spiritual healing methods; investigates whether the "Energy/Life Force" is scientific or spiritual; and describes almost 80 different Alternative Therapies, from Aromatherapy to Zone therapies. Also examines reasons why some are not healed & how to overcome these failures Biblically. Co-authored with Dr. Badu Bediako, (former Assoc. Professor of BioChemistry.) Best Seller
Book, E-book, MP4 & DVD

How to Recognize the Voice of God. How does God communicate to His people? How will you know when it is Him speaking to you? This very practical teaching has already helped many.
Book & DVD

Raising a Blessed Generation. The goals of this teaching are three-fold:
Goal 1: To understand what Blessing is and the Power it has for our lives today;
Goal 2: To Identify and Recover any missed blessings in my own life;
Goal 3: To Begin to Learn How to Bless others, especially our children & grandchildren! Identity and gender confusion is caused by the failure of parents & grandparents to speak identity and destiny into the young ones. Best Seller
Book, E-book, MP4 & DVD

Daniel and the Star Chasers. The counterfeit of Astrology has hidden what God wanted His people to know about the Gospel message in the stars. Daniel taught that truth to the Magi of Asia, and that nearly caused the War of the Continents half a millennium later. Only in recent decades has mankind had the technology to uncover what the Magi saw. Following Daniel's instructions, they went to see the King of Kings and submit their kingdoms and empires to His.
Book, E-book, MP4 & DVD

The Christian Life & the Role of the Fivefold Ministry. The Christian church is being increasingly side-lined in social debate. Have we ceased to be the Salt and Light commanded by Jesus Christ? The Solution: become real Christians! But what does that entail? Then, how are Christians to be governed? God provided the Fivefold ministry to do that. What does that look like? Best Seller
Book, E-book, MP4 & DVD

Help! The Sheep are Escaping: Understanding the Exodus From Church to God's Ecclesia. For most Christians in the West, "church" isn't working! The Old Wineskin cannot compete any longer, as God raises up His New Wineskin to fulfil His end-time purposes. The solution is for "church" to become Ecclesia and for participation with appropriate equipping, releasing and accountability.
Book, E-book, MP4 & DVD

Biblical Healing Training Manual. This thorough examination of Biblical physical healing is the result of many years of experience as well as training under some of the world's best Bible teachers. There are many "How To's", practical prayer and ministry guidelines, reasons why some aren't healed, and what we can do about them, etc. Hundreds have been healed, & many congregations have been empowered to commence regular Healing services with Christ-glorifying results. Best Seller
Book, E-book, MP4 & DVD

Fatal Faith - the Cult Counterfeit of Christianity. This book explains how cults develop and what patterns to avoid. Key Christian and Cult beliefs are compared with the main active cults. How to handle door-knockers, cult exiting, pre-cult spiritually-abusive churches; and how to protect young people from cults. Major ancient & modern heresies examined. Best Seller. *Book, E-book*

The New Age - the Old Lie in a New Package. New Age & Bible beliefs and practices compared, including Reincarnation and Past lives, Astrology, the New Age pseudo Messiah, Self-worship & our Deity-potential. Energy/ Life Forces are examined, and the occult involvement of most holistic health gurus. Best Seller
Book, E-book

Discerning the Past to See the End Times: *Islam's Role in the Return of Jesus.* The statue in Nebuchadnezzar's dream, interpreted by Daniel, gives us a clear picture of the various empires that have sought domination of the Middle East and beyond. World events circle around this area of vital interest to God and His people. The Bible is a Middle Eastern book, not a European or American book. The context of the empires of the statue give us vital clues about the Empire of the Beast to come! Best Seller
Book, E-book, MP4 & DVD

Signs & Symbols: Cult, New Age & Occult Insignias & What They Mean. From Ananda Marga, Anarchy, & Ankhs, to Yin & Yang, Yoga & Zodiacs. By popular demand this book has a brief explanation & a Biblical comparison with dozens of insignias. 7th Edition, newly revised. Best Seller
Book, E-book

How to Minister to Change Lives and Communities. This comprehensive & practical training manual is for those who want to do effective ministry. This can include end-of-service and small-group ministry. Topics include Understanding the Spiritual Realm; Empowerment to Serve; Healing of the Body, & the Soul; Deeper Ministry by appointment & referral; & Biblical blessings to release identity and destiny. Best Seller
Book, E-book, MP4 & DVD

The Bible 101. A teaching manual introducing the Bible, explaining clearly it's purposes, origins, history, inspiration, symbolism, translations & versions, moving from milk to meat, study helps, rules of interpretation, and how to study it to get the best understanding.
Book, E-book, & MP4

Unmasking Freemasonry - Removing the Hoodwink. Written primarily for the wives & families of Masons to explain the curses brought on themselves and their families through the oaths; then learn how to deal with the effects. History & structure are explained simply. A Past Master who read this book immediately resigned from his Lodge. The prayer guidelines from this book are being used by many ministries worldwide. 7th edition with endorsement by C. Peter Wagner. Best Seller
Book, E-book, MP4 & DVD

Unmasking Mormonism - Who are the Latter-day Saints? Learn about LDS founder Joseph Smith on whose credentials this cult fails Bible tests, the Book of Mormon hoax, Mormon polytheism, true & false priesthood & authority. This book has caused many Mormons to cancel their baptisms & leave to seek the genuine Jesus Christ - the One from the Bible. Best Seller
Book, E-book, MP4 & DVD

Unmasking the Watchtower - Who are the Jehovah's Witnesses? This asks the questions many J.W.'s are being expelled for daring to ask! Check out the changeable prophecies and man-made doctrines of the Watchtower, the authoritarian leaders & their use of Mind-Control & manipulation of members, how to know the One True God, and how you can witness to and pray for a J.W. effectively. Best Seller
Book, E-book, MP4 & DVD

Rome's Anathemas: Insights into the Papal Pantheon. This vital book investigates Constantine's divorce of the Jewish roots of the Christian faith and its replacement with paganism; the Council of Trent rejected the Biblical basis of Luther's Reformation and cursed all who disagreed with them. In John, we read of the marriage feast at Cana. Realizing that the wine was gone and that she herself could not do anything, Mary tells Jesus, because He is the only One who could do something. Mary then gives the stewards her last recorded words and only command - one that we must consider for us to be saved. Mary said, *"Whatever He say to you, do it!"*
Book, E-book, MP4 & DVD

Additional Resources Available by
Selwyn R. Stevens
www.jubileeresources.org (Webshop)
Plus comprehensive range of free tracts to download

Made in the USA
Columbia, SC
10 September 2024

41547413R00076